*Also available in this series (ti*

**D0608451**

To Alan and Pete for being
there when the going got
tough.

# Psychology and Work

*Christine Hodson*

## SOUTH CHESHIRE COLLEGE
## CENTRAL LRC

Acc no. A00 14174

Date 11/04 Price 9.99 Supplier L·D

Invoice No.

Order No. 1R 24137

Class no. 158.7

First published 2001
by Routledge
27 Church Road, Hove, E. Sussex, BN3 2FA
Simultaneously published in the USA and Canada
by Taylor & Francis Inc.,
29 West 35th Street, New York, NY 10001
*Routledge is an imprint of the Taylor & Francis Group*

© 2001 Christine Hodson

Typeset in Times by Keystroke,
Jacaranda Lodge, Wolverhampton
Printed and bound in Great Britain
by TJ International Ltd, Padstow, Cornwall

All rights reserved. No part of this book may be reprinted
or reproduced or utilised in any form or by any electronic, mechanical,
or other means, now known or hereafter invented, including
photocopying and recording, or in any information storage or
retrieval system, without permission in writing from the publishers.

*British Library Cataloguing-in-Publication Data*
A catalogue record for this book is available from the British Library

*Library of Congress Cataloging in Publication Data*
Hodson, Christine, 1940–
  Psychology and work / Christine Hodson.
    p. cm. – (Routledge modular psychology)
  Includes bibliographical references and index.
  ISBN 0-415-22773-9 – ISBN 0-415-22774-7 (pbk.)
  1. Work–Psychological aspects. I. Title. II. Series.

BF481 .H63 2001
158.7–dc21                                          2001031922

ISBN 0–415–22773–9 (hbk)
ISBN 0–415–22774–7 (pbk)

# Contents

# Illustrations

# Acknowledgements

Christine Hodson and Routledge acknowledge the expert help of Phil Banyard at OCR and Christine Brain at Edexcel in compiling the Study Aids Chapter.

OCR examination questions are reproduced by permission of Oxford Cambridge and RSA Examinations. OCR and Edexcel do not accept responsibility for either the answers or the examiners' comments in the Study Aids chapter of this or any other book in the series.

The author would like to thank Alan Jones, Peter Jones and Louisa King for the advice and practical help offered during the writing of the book, particularly in dealing with the tantrums of an ancient computer, and to her partner Mick Newman for his support and patience. Grateful thanks are also due to the series editors, Cara Flanagan and Phil Banyard, and to Rachel Brazil at Routledge for their invaluable advice and guidance.

the labour market and school was mainly regarded as a preparation for work. In the 1950s, when the school-leaving age was raised to 15 years, only 15 per cent of children stayed on after this age in order to study, the vast majority went straight into work with only a minority of these working children receiving any day-release training.

> Young people must now stay in the education system until they are 16 years old. Most now stay on until they are 18 years old. Is this appropriate for everyone? Should the system be more flexible? Suggest two ways in which the system could be more flexible and discuss the implications for society. You may like to consider prolonged periods of work experience or lowering the school-leaving age.

## men and work

Women formed a vital part of the workforce during the industrial revolution, working alongside men in the factories. Many were also employed in domestic service to keep the large households of the upper and middle classes functioning. However most upper- and middle-class women did not have paid employment and it was expected that they would be kept by either their husband, father or other male relative. By the beginning of the twentieth century a working woman was regarded as a sign of poverty or non-conformity. Except in areas such as northern England, where women worked in factories, working-class women who did work were most likely to be employed in a domestic capacity. As the century progressed women increasingly entered the workforce, particularly to do men's jobs during the two great European wars. By the 1930s it had become acceptable for single women to work but they were expected to give up their jobs automatically if they married. In 1944 the government passed legislation preventing education authorities from dismissing teachers for getting married, while trainee nurses were required to leave their training if they married until as recently as the 1970s.

It was also common for women to be paid less than men for doing the same job. Work, therefore, was something that was essential and worthwhile for men but peripheral or perverse for women. Even though

# 1

# Introduction

Historical approaches to work
Organisational psychology
Summary

When we meet a new person one of the first questions we are likely to ask is 'What do you do?' Work, or more accurately paid employment, is central to an adult individual's identity in Western society. Michael Portillo, the Conservative member of parliament who lost his seat in the 1997 general election, told *The Observer* (*Guardian* 1999) 'I have that normal male thing of valuing myself according to the job I do . . . When I can't tell someone in one word what I am, then something is missing. I don't represent anything any more'.

Whilst work is obviously more than paid employment and includes housework, do-it-yourself, unpaid caring and voluntary work, it is used by the Government to define our social class and by advertisers to predict our patterns of expenditure. Those who do not work are often defined by the job of their spouse or the job they had before they gave up work. It is not surprising that this is an area where psychological theory has been extensively applied in recent years. The aim of this text is to explore the impact of employment and unemployment on the individual and to look at the ways in which psychology has been applied in the workplace. The whole area is often referred to as the Psychology of Organisations and many of the findings can be applied in non-work settings, for example to sports teams.

In our present society it is expected that most individuals will join the labour market when they complete full-time education and will depend upon paid work for their main source of income until they retire. Adults who do not work are viewed unfavourably unless they have an independent income or are actively involved in caring for children or dependent relatives. Freud (1938) stated that the hallmarks of good mental health were 'to love and to work'.

However the idea that all adults should be in paid employment is recent and can only be applied in industrialised societies. In non-industrialised societies individuals or families are largely self-supporting. They may work to produce goods or services for them-selves and sell or barter the surplus with others. The word work, as we understand it, may not exist although there would be language to describe specific tasks such as gathering crops. The current pattern of the majority of the population being workers in the employ of others rather than being self-sufficient is a product of industrialisation and is less than 250 years old.

## Historical approaches to work

In ancient Greece and Rome work, particularly tasks involving manual labour, was performed by slaves and a large unit such as a farm would be staffed by a team of slaves under the guidance of family members. This pattern was still evident in the Middle Ages when the members of the church and the nobility believed that manual tasks were only appropriate for people of lower status. As an example, a serf would owe a certain number of days work to the Lord of the Manor but a yeoman or freeman, who had higher status, would have no such obligation. This does not mean that work was not an important source of identity and status. The craft guilds, such as cordwainers who made shoes, became extremely powerful in the Middle Ages because of their members' skills. The craft skills were known as mysteries and current usage of the word may give an indication as to their historical status and importance. Many family names, for example Smith, Taylor and Cooper, are derived from the jobs people did.

### The industrial re▮

It was not until advances in technology triggered the Industr▮ Revolution that the pattern of long-term, full-time work for wages, the employ of another person, developed. Before this time work▮ were hired on a temporary basis, sometimes annually but frequen▮ seasonally. This is still the case in agricultural areas in the UK, wh▮ workers are still hired for the fruit and vegetable-picking seasons. O▮ people moved to work in large units such as factories, the beginni▮ of our modern pattern of needing a job to provide sufficient resou▮ for the individual and their dependants, rather than being self-suffic▮ began to emerge. These early workers, who had often moved from▮ home areas to live near a factory, or who worked in gangs buil▮ railways and canals, had a fearsome reputation. They were poorly▮ and their working conditions were highly unsatisfactory and frequ▮ unsafe. It was common for a 60-hour week to be worked, with S▮ as the only day of rest. The workers, who included men, wome▮ children, were seen as idle and prone to violence and drunke▮ Although they would only be paid when they were actually a▮ absenteeism was rife. Employers were harsh and there was little▮ for the welfare of workers, who were frequently viewed as mere▮ unit of cost, to be hired and fired as necessary. As the nineteenth ▮ progressed some employers became concerned by these conditi▮ several model factory and village communities, such as Saltaire▮ Yorkshire, were established where the welfare of the workers▮ a priority.

### Child▮

As the nineteenth century progressed employment patterns▮ change. Children, who had been employed in many of the lea▮ and most poorly paid areas, were progressively excluded fr▮ jobs. Full-time compulsory education was introduced in 18▮ was partly because of the realisation that workers needed to ▮ and numerate. This was the beginning of the links between ▮ and work that are still apparent. For example, at the turn of th▮ in Lancashire it was quite common for girls, once they re▮ age of 11 years, to do half a day in the factory and half a day▮ The aims of education were often interpreted in terms of th▮

most women now work many of them are in part-time employment whilst most men work full time. Over 40 per cent of the women who work in the UK are employed on a part-time basis whereas this figure for men is about 6 per cent. Part-time work is often still viewed as being 'not a proper job', unless it is professional work.

### Male employment patterns

Patterns of employment for the male worker have also changed. Prior to and during the Industrial Revolution the majority of male workers performed manual jobs. Those with a high level of skill had the highest wages and a gap in status emerged between skilled and non-skilled operatives. Jobs in highly skilled or highly paid areas were often kept in families and the apprenticeship system became an effective gateway to the more skilled and highly paid manual jobs.

The second half of the twentieth century has seen a move away from industrial employment for males towards office and service industry jobs. This process is still continuing and the total number of jobs in manufacturing has fallen from one third to one quarter of all employment between 1991 and 1998. As office and service industry jobs were often seen as women's work this has meant a shift in the definition and meaning of work. This move away from physical jobs such as mining and heavy engineering, to service, clerical and information technology jobs is referred to as the **feminisation** of the workforce. An example of this process is found in clerical work. In 1911 80 per cent of clerks were men and the job was a highly respected route into professional employment for working- and lower-middle-class young men. As Gilbert and Sullivan pointed out in *HMS Pinafore* one could go a long way progressing from clerical work and 'polishing the knocker on the big front door'. By 1971 71 per cent of clerks were women. Clerical work had become a low status job and was often seen as something done for 'pin money' rather than a working wage.

### Links between employment and education

The aims of education have become more closely allied to the needs of the labour market. There is a gap in terms of employment opportunities between those with academic qualifications and those without, and this gap is getting wider. I suspect that the main reason most of you are reading this book is in order to obtain a qualification which will, in turn, help your employment prospects!

Over the last 10 years the gap between the rewards for those with highly prized skills and those who are either semi- or unskilled has widened considerably. The former **group** often change jobs or may become self-employed whilst the latter group are at greater risk of periods of unemployment. The labour market has become increasingly individualistic and job security is becoming rarer. Most politicians are proud to announce that 'jobs for life have gone'. The belief is that the pace of technological change is so rapid that the workforce needs to be 'flexible' and open to retraining to ensure continuing economic prosperity.

Progress exercise

Identify three ways in which **attitudes** towards work have changed over the past 150 years, concentrating on the way these changes have affected a) men, b) women and c) children.

## Organisational psychology

**Organisational psychology** has been defined by Carlson (1988: 12) as 'A branch of psychology involved in industry that advises management about the application of psychological principles to running a business' and by Riggio (1990) as 'The branch of Psychology that is concerned with the study of behaviour in work settings and the application of psychological principles to changing work behaviour.'

Organisational psychology must be seen in the social, historical and cultural context described earlier in this chapter. It began to emerge as a specific application of psychology in the UK in the 1920s and the first company to appoint what was then known as an industrial psychologist was Rowntree in 1922. Reflecting employment patterns at the time **industrial psychology's** main concerns were the patterns of working and management and labour relations in large factories, such as car-manufacturing plants. Whilst some employers, for example

# Introduction

 Historical approaches to work
Organisational psychology
Summary

When we meet a new person one of the first questions we are likely to ask is 'What do you do?' Work, or more accurately paid employment, is central to an adult individual's identity in Western society. Michael Portillo, the Conservative member of parliament who lost his seat in the 1997 general election, told *The Observer* (*Guardian* 1999) 'I have that normal male thing of valuing myself according to the job I do . . . When I can't tell someone in one word what I am, then something is missing. I don't represent anything any more'.

Whilst work is obviously more than paid employment and includes housework, do-it-yourself, unpaid caring and voluntary work, it is used by the Government to define our social class and by advertisers to predict our patterns of expenditure. Those who do not work are often defined by the job of their spouse or the job they had before they gave up work. It is not surprising that this is an area where psychological theory has been extensively applied in recent years. The aim of this text is to explore the impact of employment and unemployment on the individual and to look at the ways in which psychology has been applied in the workplace. The whole area is often referred to as the Psychology of Organisations and many of the findings can be applied in non-work settings, for example to sports teams.

In our present society it is expected that most individuals will join the labour market when they complete full-time education and will depend upon paid work for their main source of income until they retire. Adults who do not work are viewed unfavourably unless they have an independent income or are actively involved in caring for children or dependent relatives. Freud (1938) stated that the hallmarks of good mental health were 'to love and to work'.

However the idea that all adults should be in paid employment is recent and can only be applied in industrialised societies. In non-industrialised societies individuals or families are largely self-supporting. They may work to produce goods or services for themselves and sell or barter the surplus with others. The word work, as we understand it, may not exist although there would be language to describe specific tasks such as gathering crops. The current pattern of the majority of the population being workers in the employ of others rather than being self-sufficient is a product of industrialisation and is less than 250 years old.

## Historical approaches to work

In ancient Greece and Rome work, particularly tasks involving manual labour, was performed by slaves and a large unit such as a farm would be staffed by a team of slaves under the guidance of family members. This pattern was still evident in the Middle Ages when the members of the church and the nobility believed that manual tasks were only appropriate for people of lower status. As an example, a serf would owe a certain number of days work to the Lord of the Manor but a yeoman or freeman, who had higher status, would have no such obligation. This does not mean that work was not an important source of identity and status. The craft guilds, such as cordwainers who made shoes, became extremely powerful in the Middle Ages because of their members' skills. The craft skills were known as mysteries and current usage of the word may give an indication as to their historical status and importance. Many family names, for example Smith, Taylor and Cooper, are derived from the jobs people did.

### The industrial revolution

It was not until advances in technology triggered the Industrial Revolution that the pattern of long-term, full-time work for wages, in the employ of another person, developed. Before this time workers were hired on a temporary basis, sometimes annually but frequently seasonally. This is still the case in agricultural areas in the UK, where workers are still hired for the fruit and vegetable-picking seasons. Once people moved to work in large units such as factories, the beginnings of our modern pattern of needing a job to provide sufficient resources for the individual and their dependants, rather than being self-sufficient, began to emerge. These early workers, who had often moved from their home areas to live near a factory, or who worked in gangs building railways and canals, had a fearsome reputation. They were poorly paid and their working conditions were highly unsatisfactory and frequently unsafe. It was common for a 60-hour week to be worked, with Sunday as the only day of rest. The workers, who included men, women and children, were seen as idle and prone to violence and drunkenness. Although they would only be paid when they were actually at work absenteeism was rife. Employers were harsh and there was little regard for the welfare of workers, who were frequently viewed as merely one unit of cost, to be hired and fired as necessary. As the nineteenth century progressed some employers became concerned by these conditions and several model factory and village communities, such as Saltaire in West Yorkshire, were established where the welfare of the workers became a priority.

### Children and work

As the nineteenth century progressed employment patterns began to change. Children, who had been employed in many of the least skilled and most poorly paid areas, were progressively excluded from many jobs. Full-time compulsory education was introduced in 1870. This was partly because of the realisation that workers needed to be literate and numerate. This was the beginning of the links between education and work that are still apparent. For example, at the turn of the century in Lancashire it was quite common for girls, once they reached the age of 11 years, to do half a day in the factory and half a day at school. The aims of education were often interpreted in terms of the needs of the labour market and school was mainly regarded as a preparation for work. In the 1950s, when the school-leaving age was raised to 15 years, only 15 per cent of children stayed on after this age in order to study, the vast majority went straight into work with only a minority of these working children receiving any day-release training.

**Progress exercise**

Young people must now stay in the education system until they are 16 years old. Most now stay on until they are 18 years old. Is this appropriate for everyone? Should the system be more flexible? Suggest two ways in which the system could be more flexible and discuss the implications for society. You may like to consider prolonged periods of work experience or lowering the school-leaving age.

## *Women and work*

Women formed a vital part of the workforce during the industrial revolution, working alongside men in the factories. Many were also employed in domestic service to keep the large households of the upper and middle classes functioning. However most upper- and middle-class women did not have paid employment and it was expected that they would be kept by either their husband, father or other male relative. By the beginning of the twentieth century a working woman was regarded as a sign of poverty or non-conformity. Except in areas such as northern England, where women worked in factories, working-class women who did work were most likely to be employed in a domestic capacity. As the century progressed women increasingly entered the workforce, particularly to do men's jobs during the two great European wars. By the 1930s it had become acceptable for single women to work but they were expected to give up their jobs automatically if they married. In 1944 the government passed legislation preventing education authorities from dismissing teachers for getting married, while trainee nurses were required to leave their training if they married until as recently as the 1970s.

It was also common for women to be paid less than men for doing the same job. Work, therefore, was something that was essential and worthwhile for men but peripheral or perverse for women. Even though most women now work many of them are in part-time employment whilst most men work full time. Over 40 per cent of the women who work in the UK are employed on a part-time basis whereas this figure for men is about 6 per cent. Part-time work is often still viewed as being 'not a proper job', unless it is professional work.

## Male employment patterns

Patterns of employment for the male worker have also changed. Prior to and during the Industrial Revolution the majority of male workers performed manual jobs. Those with a high level of skill had the highest wages and a gap in status emerged between skilled and non-skilled operatives. Jobs in highly skilled or highly paid areas were often kept in families and the apprenticeship system became an effective gateway to the more skilled and highly paid manual jobs.

The second half of the twentieth century has seen a move away from industrial employment for males towards office and service industry jobs. This process is still continuing and the total number of jobs in manufacturing has fallen from one third to one quarter of all employment between 1991 and 1998. As office and service industry jobs were often seen as women's work this has meant a shift in the definition and meaning of work. This move away from physical jobs such as mining and heavy engineering, to service, clerical and information technology jobs is referred to as the **feminisation** of the workforce. An example of this process is found in clerical work. In 1911 80 per cent of clerks were men and the job was a highly respected route into professional employment for working- and lower-middle-class young men. As Gilbert and Sullivan pointed out in *HMS Pinafore* one could go a long way progressing from clerical work and 'polishing the knocker on the big front door'. By 1971 71 per cent of clerks were women. Clerical work had become a low status job and was often seen as something done for 'pin money' rather than a working wage.

## Links between employment and education

The aims of education have become more closely allied to the needs of the labour market. There is a gap in terms of employment opportunities between those with academic qualifications and those without, and this gap is getting wider. I suspect that the main reason most of you are reading this book is in order to obtain a qualification which will, in turn, help your employment prospects!

Over the last 10 years the gap between the rewards for those with highly prized skills and those who are either semi- or unskilled has widened considerably. The former **group** often change jobs or may become self-employed whilst the latter group are at greater risk of periods of unemployment. The labour market has become increasingly individualistic and job security is becoming rarer. Most politicians are proud to announce that 'jobs for life have gone'. The belief is that the pace of technological change is so rapid that the workforce needs to be 'flexible' and open to retraining to ensure continuing economic prosperity.

**Progress exercise**

Identify three ways in which **attitudes** towards work have changed over the past 150 years, concentrating on the way these changes have affected a) men, b) women and c) children.

## Organisational psychology

**Organisational psychology** has been defined by Carlson (1988: 12) as 'A branch of psychology involved in industry that advises management about the application of psychological principles to running a business' and by Riggio (1990) as 'The branch of Psychology that is concerned with the study of behaviour in work settings and the application of psychological principles to changing work behaviour.'

Organisational psychology must be seen in the social, historical and cultural context described earlier in this chapter. It began to emerge as a specific application of psychology in the UK in the 1920s and the first company to appoint what was then known as an industrial psychologist was Rowntree in 1922. Reflecting employment patterns at the time **industrial psychology's** main concerns were the patterns of working and management and labour relations in large factories, such as car-manufacturing plants. Whilst some employers, for example

Rowntree, employed psychologists to improve the lot of their workers and encouraged consultation, others employed them purely with the aim of improving profits and productivity. Consequently the discipline has had a mixed press!

Frederick Taylor (1911) was an engineer who was concerned with improving the level of productivity in factories in the USA. Using a scientific approach and much influenced by the work of the early behaviourists (see pp. 24–26) he published a seminal text *The Principles of Scientific Management* which laid great emphasis on efficient workplace organisation, appropriate selection and training of employees and applying what he called common-sense principles in the workplace. The central features in his approach were

- time and motion studies to ensure that working methods adopted were as efficient and productive as possible
- the use of piece rates rather than paying all workers the same regardless of their productivity
- training supervisors (or foremen as they were then called) to supervise more effectively and to plan and check on shop-floor performance.

Many of these practices have been widely adopted, although the approach has been criticised for presuming that financial rewards are of prime importance. It is often referred to as the 'stick and carrot' model.

With the change in employment patterns in recent years industrial psychology now concerns itself with all types of organisations and is applied to both blue- and white-collar settings. The discipline is now known as organisational psychology rather than industrial psychology. Whilst it places the relationships between workers and management at its centre, the findings of organisational psychology are now also applied to other settings such as the armed forces, voluntary agencies and sports teams. By 1991 there were 30,000 organisational psychologists in the European Union. In the UK organisational psychology is now a separate branch of the British Psychological Society and is known in this context as **occupational psychology**. Until recently research in organisational psychology has been based on a predominantly male perspective and is dominated by academic research published in English. It has little to say about self-employment and has only recently begun to explore cultural differences and the role of organisations in non-western settings. The main aim of this book is to examine the impact of employment, or lack of it, on the individual and to introduce organisational psychology to new readers.

**Review exercise**

Outline the development of organisational psychology this century. Why do you think that it developed alongside large organisations and is mostly concerned with the structure of organisations rather than individual workers?

## Summary

This chapter has attempted to define what is meant by work and has briefly outlined the history of attitudes to work in western society. Work was seen as central to identity in the twentieth century. Children have been progressively removed from the workforce over the past 130 years and spend more time in education. The increasing involvement of women in paid employment during the twentieth century was examined. It was noted that the employment prospects and wages of females are still inferior to those of male workers. The implications of the scientific management of changes from blue- to white-collar working for men and the notion of the feminisation of work were introduced. The links between education and work were discussed. The organisational or industrial society has been defined and its development over the twentieth century has been discussed.

## Further reading

Furnham, A. (1990) *The Protestant Work Ethic*, London: Routledge. A history of attitudes to work in the western world. As the text is written by a psychologist it provides useful and relevant background material.

Statt, D.A. (1994) *Psychology and the World of Work*, Basingstoke: Macmillan. This book gives an overview of the study of work in the twentieth century from a **psychodynamic** perspective. You may not agree with the approach but it is not as hampered by jargon and technical terms as some other texts.

# 2

# The significance of work to the individual

## Introduction

Although someone once asked 'If work is such a good thing why do the rich not keep it to themselves?' there is evidence that some people, such as lottery winners, feel lost if they give up work and you may be familiar with the proverb 'The devil finds work for idle hands'. As stated in Chapter 1, work is seen as being central to a person's identity in western society. The significance of work lies not just in being in employment but also in the nature and description of the job and the status the job confers on the individual.

It should be apparent from the first chapter that there are differing attitudes to different types of work. Professional jobs, such as those in medicine or law, are regarded in a different way to unskilled labour and factory work. The old-fashioned terminology for this is **white-collar** and **blue-collar** work. The government, using the Registrar General's categories, classifies professional and white-collar jobs as social classes 1, 2 and 3a, and blue-collar jobs as 3b, 4 and 5. Advertising agencies use similar categories. Managers are treated in a different way to workers and most organisational psychology literature is aimed at managers, to enable them to manage or supervise workers.

In many workplaces in the UK, workers and management have separate eating areas. In the police force and in some branches of the armed forces promotion from a worker's grade to a management grade means that the individual concerned must work in a different setting. These practices imply that managers and workers are very different and the difference is so fundamental that, if a worker is promoted, they can not manage their peers. It is interesting that this does not always occur in professional settings where the staff in lower ranking posts are known as juniors, interns or trainees, and are treated accordingly. Attitudes to work reflect the values society places on particular types of employment and they are not consistent. For example the relationship between a hospital administrator and a junior doctor will be different to the relationship between the same administrator and a domestic supervisor. This reflects the historical and cultural background discussed in the previous chapter. As the text progresses we will explore some of the implications of these attitudes.

It is useful, therefore, to focus on the significance and meaning of work to both the individual involved and wider society. Peter Warr created a valuable psychological model which looks at the importance of work for the psychological well-being of an individual.

## Warr's vitamin model

Peter Warr (1987) proposed nine **determinants** of mental health in all environments and applied these to all working and organisational settings. Figure 2.1 presents a list of these determinants, or factors, which determine psychological health. His theory could be applied more generally but he was most concerned with the significance of work in maintaining the individual's mental and physical health in modern western society.

Let us examine Warr's model in some detail. Its historical roots lie in studies produced by psychologists and sociologists who examined the effect of the economic depression on individuals and communities in the UK in the 1920s and 1930s, and suggested that the effect on both was harmful. This led to the development of theories about effects of employment and unemployment upon the individual. More recently Warr (1987) suggested that mental health is determined by an inter-

Peter Warr's vitamin model:

Environmental influences on mental health

1. Opportunity for control
2. Opportunity for skill use
3. Externally generated goals
4. Variety
5. Environmental clarity
6. Availability of money
7. Physical security
8. Opportunity for social contact
9. Valued social position

*Figure 2.1* **Warr's vitamin model**

action between the individual and their environment and that, in present-day society, work is one aspect of the environment that has a highly important influence. He listed nine determinants of psychological well-being and likened these determinants to vitamins. In the same way that a lack of a vitamins in the diet can cause physical illness, such as a deficiency of vitamin C resulting in scurvy, some environmental factors can have similar results for psychological health. Work is instrumental in assisting individuals to provide these factors for themselves and their dependants, being unable to find a job or losing the job you have can result in poverty, homelessness and low social status, resulting in a lowering of self-esteem. The determinants are examined below under headings which indicate the effect Warr believes they have upon the individual and are not examined in the order they appear in the figure.

*Constant effect determinants*

Warr labelled three determinants as **constant effect determinants** (CE). These are

- availability of money
- physical security
- valued social position.

It may be possible for an individual to have too much of these factors in their life, and the absence of these three factors will have a detrimental effect on the individual's mental and physical health. Therefore their presence can be said to have a positive effect on health and their absence a negative effect.

To make the position clearer we will now look at each of these factors in detail.

*Availability of money* Most individuals and families obtain money either by working or from pensions and savings built up during employment. If an individual cannot work they are likely to have no money and will have to rely on state benefits, which are very low, or on charity from others. Poverty, i.e. not having enough money to keep oneself and one's dependants, is obviously damaging. In western industrialised environments a low income may enable individuals to survive but it results in a lack of the choices that are available to individuals with more resources. Poverty has been linked to both poor mental and physical health.

*Physical security* By this Warr means a safe living environment which presents reasonably permanent security of tenure. The safe living environment should provide security from physical threat, it should be warm or cool enough as required, and have space to prepare and serve food. In western society a safe living environment is also expected to provide personal space for privacy and a secure place to keep one's belongings. One need only look at the plight of refugees or the victims of natural disasters to realise how important physical security is.

*Valued social position* Humans are a social species, i.e. they live in groups. A person's position in the social structure is important and high self-esteem comes from being valued by others within the social structure. At any given time each individual may be a part of several different social structures and may be of different status in different groups. Employment offers one opportunity for high social status, derived either from skills held or from a high position in a hierarchical structure. The prospect of low status appears if the job is perceived as undesirable or the individual is at the bottom of the structure. If the job is removed or no work is available then a readjustment has to take place, resulting in a possible drop in self-esteem. As stated in Chapter 1, an individual's social position depends on employment and most unemployed people are of low status. A situation which is perhaps encapsulated by the statement 'well, I'm only a housewife' with all that that infers!

The other six determinants are essential for health but, like some vitamins, can cause damage if you get too much of them. As an analogy, we can think of vitamin D. This vitamin is necessary to prevent rickets but excessive amounts can disrupt the balance of basic chemicals, such as calcium and phosphates, in the body leading to serious problems. The other items on Warr's list are therefore essential but need to be in the right balance. These are described as AD, for **additional decrement**, meaning that we need enough of them but an excess can have deleterious effects. They fall into two sub-groups.

The first group is

- opportunity for control
- opportunity for skill use
- opportunity for social contact.

The second group is

- externally generated goals
- variety
- **environmental clarity**.

If these determinants are examined one by one the position will become clearer.

*Opportunity for control* One of the basic beliefs in psychology is that we need to feel in control of our environment and ourselves, and that feelings of lack of control are implicated in depression and other mental disorders. Warr acknowledges this. Since being in control of our working environment improves our sense of worth, problems can occur when an individual has no control over their environment or is pressed into constant decision making without time to consider the consequences. Also there are occasions when the individual must make decisions but is unable to predict their outcome. In some jobs and professions, for example dealing with futures on the stock exchange or working with people with behaviour difficulties, this is an integral part of the job. These jobs are notorious for **burnout** where people are made ill by the demands of their job. We will return to this area when we look at health and work in Chapter 5.

*Opportunity for skill use* Being able to perform a skilled job successfully, such as carpentry or fashion designing, can lead to high levels of personal satisfaction and high self-esteem. Having to work in environments where your skills are unused or undervalued is demoralising. There is evidence that when skills, which have taken many years to develop, are no longer required, depression may result amongst the older redundant workers. Not only has the job gone but also the individual's identity is undermined. This was highly apparent in 'railway' towns such as Swindon when the manufacture of engines and carriages ceased. However being asked to use extremely complex skills for prolonged periods can lead to overload and burnout.

*Opportunity for social contact* Most people are aware of the damaging effects of social isolation. Similarly we are aware of the effects of overcrowding and most of us will avoid such environments or try to restrict our time in them. In some jobs this is impossible, for example working in a customer service environment, where there is both constant contact with people and angry customers to be placated, can be very stressful.

*Externally generated goals* Externally generated goals give a structure to the working day, and achieving goals at work or in other settings can give us a sense of self-worth and increase our feelings of being 'in control'. If the goals become impossible to accomplish, either because there are too many or they make unreasonable demands on our resources and skills, then they may become damaging. Setting unrealistic targets for oneself or having them imposed from outside, can create an unpleasant working environment and lead to personal distress. This is closely linked to the issue of control.

*Variety* This is also known as the 'spice of life'. We all need change and stimulation in our environment and will seek it out if it is not available. However an environment which constantly changes, particularly in ways which can not be predicted, can be harmful to both physical and mental health.

*Environmental clarity* This concept is central to Warr's theory and may at first seem more difficult to understand. Warr describes it as 'the degree to which a person's environment is clear or opaque' and he states that it has three aspects.

1. The first one is the availability of feedback about the consequences of actions. Our knowledge of who we are is, at least in part, a product of the way others react to our behaviour. An individual who does not know whether their actions are correct or incorrect, acceptable or unacceptable, will find the environment increasingly unpredictable and potentially frightening.
2. The second is the predictability of the people and environment which the individual encounters. We become anxious if we do not know how individuals will respond to us or if we have to deal with new systems. The fear that many experienced workers show when new technology is introduce is a good example of this. Think back to your first few days at college or in a new job and remember how confusing things were.
3. The third factor is the social and normative expectations about roles and behaviour. Do we know what is expected of us in any given social situation? We have probably all experienced nerves when asked to face a new social situation, even if we are looking forward to it. Alternatively, a totally predictable environment where things change rarely, if at all, can pose its own problems. Goffman (1961) illustrated this very clearly in his study of large institutions. The long-term unemployed can reach an emotional state where they become resigned to their position and adopt a view that they will never work again which can cause apathy, withdrawal and depression.

Using Warr's model discuss *three* factors which illustrate the importance of work in adult life.

Progress exercise

## Commentary on the vitamin model

The vitamin model provides a useful overview of the potential costs and benefits of work but it has its limitations. Warr is aware that most of the research that was available when he first published his theory concerned male workers and that work may have a different significance and meaning for women. The research is also concerned mainly with material from the USA, Europe and Australasia. It is important to recognise that theory in organisational psychology is influenced by social and cultural differences.

### Support for the model

The model is based on extensive research that Warr (1987) collected from his own studies and others completed in Holland, Australia and the USA. For example Warr and Jackson (1985) demonstrated links between unemployment and low self-esteem. On the other hand males, who were principal wage earners, reported high levels of personal satisfaction and self-esteem to Bradburn (1969). Moser *et al.* (1984) analysed mortality data for males aged 15 to 64 years in the UK over a 10-year period from 1971 to 1981. The unemployed men in the study showed a greater mortality rate, that is they died at a younger age, than those in employment. Dooley and Catalano (1984) in a study of unemployment in Los Angeles, found that self-reports of general distress and physical illness occurred after 2 months of unemployment. The effects were greater in the middle classes than in working classes. Beale and Nethercott's study (1985) also demonstrates clear links between job loss and health. This area will be discussed in greater detail in Chapter 5, Health and Work.

### Criticism of the model

On the negative side there are many problems with the theory. For example, the central notion of environmental clarity is particularly difficult to quantify and assess in any meaningful way. Also, as Warr (1987) himself pointed out, there are huge differences between individuals. This means that the determinants will be perceived differently by different people and by the same person at different points in their life cycle.

It is also impossible to disentangle the effects of separate determinants. Whilst it is clear that the availability of money and physical security are basic needs some of the other determinants are more difficult to quantify. For example 'status' or 'valued social' position at work may be of overwhelming importance in settings such as politics or the armed forces but may be of little consequence to a student working part time in a retail setting. There is an increasing tendency in western society for monetary reward to be used as a status symbol. Some individuals prize social contacts at work and will turn down promotion if they feel that it will jeopardise these contacts, while others have little or no regard for their fellows and view promotion as a priority. In Chapter 3 Maslow's theory of **motivation**, which places needs in a hierarchical structure, will be discussed and you may wish to compare this theory with Warr's model.

## McGregor's X and Y types of workers

McGregor's model (1960) is an earlier and equally influential model for understanding the meaning of work. This model differentiates between *two* sets of assumptions and expectations which managers have about employees. They represent two opposing sets of beliefs about the workforce and, as will be seen, are directly related to the historical attitudes to work in western industrialised societies discussed in Chapter 1. Warr's work started from the workers' point of view. McGregor's prime focus was the view of managers.

*Theory X and Theory Y*

**Theory X** assumes that those who work for others generally find the experience aversive. It presumes that the majority of the population would prefer idleness to work.

**Theory Y** presumes that work is an activity that the majority of people enjoy and that they prefer it to idleness.

We will now examine these two theories and their assumptions in greater detail.

Theory X assumes

• that people basically do not like working and will avoid it if possible

- that whilst at work the individual wants to avoid responsibility and needs to be directed
- that people must be coerced and, if necessary, threatened to achieve the goals of the organisation
- that money is a powerful motivator
- that job security is more important than personal achievement and job satisfaction.

Theory Y assumes

- that people can enjoy work because it is a natural activity
- that people can and will seek out and accept responsibility
- that people need not be coerced, in fact they will exercise self-direction if they understand and are committed to the goals of the organisation
- that rewards are more effective than punishment in obtaining the best from the workforce
- that most people have untapped potentials and that organisations fail to make full use of them.

McGregor's model stated that these underlying beliefs would be instrumental in deciding management strategy within organisations.

### Commentary on McGregor's model

It was an extremely influential model and much management theory has used McGregor as a starting point. Theory X would anticipate constant conflict between managers and workers as the managers' task would be to force unwilling workers to complete their jobs when they did not wish to do so. Theory Y would assume that managers and workers shared common goals and interests and would therefore co-operate. In Chapter 7 the notion of task-orientated and people-oriented strategies in managing groups will be discussed. Task orientation is related to the Theory X view and people orientation to the Theory Y view.

Theory X can be applied to workers and Theory Y to professionals and managers. Theory X can be seen as a continuation of the beliefs about the early factory workers in Victorian times, whereas Theory Y is a continuation of the classical and medieval attitudes which valued intellectual tasks and despised manual labour. This would confirm previous statements about cultural and social differences, as the theory is reflective of the 1950s and 1960s when the model was created. During this period confrontation between managers and workers was seen as inevitable by both sides. It could be argued that Theory X workers are the product of boring, routine and undervalued jobs and Theory Y workers are the product of interesting, fulfilling high-status jobs. In fairness to McGregor he did not state that these were just two of the perspectives which managers *might* have. He did not say they were the *only* two which exist.

Theory Y is closer to Warr and assumes that work can be a positive experience for almost everyone and that it can have much to offer. This reflects the changes in attitude in management theory that started in the 1960s and it shows the influence of the work of Maslow which is discussed in Chapter 3.

> Describe and evaluate both McGregor's and Warr's models. Is work essential to good mental and emotional health or not?
>
> Review exercise

## Summary

This chapter has looked at the meaning of work for the individual and has explored the difference in attitudes to professional and manual work. It has given an overview of Warr's nine factors, suggesting that work can be an important determinant of mental health. These determinants are separated into constant effect determinants which cannot exist in excess, and additional decrement determinants which can become damaging if they exist in excess. McGregor's Type X and Type Y workers, are opposing types of worker with Type X being negative and Type Y positive. It was pointed out that this theory is based on work with males in western societies.

## Further reading

Warr, P.B. (1987) *Work, Unemployment and Mental Health*, Oxford: Oxford University Press. This text contains a detailed explanation from Warr. It is a seminal text which has had a good deal of influence on social policy, it is worth persevering with it if you want an in-depth analysis of the area.

McGregor, D. (1960) *The Human Side of Enterprise*, New York: McGraw-Hill. A text which has been highly influential. It is interesting as an example of the popularisation of psychological theory in management. The text is designed for managers rather than students.

# Motivation at work

## Introduction

One of the main concerns of organisational psychology is to discover the motivation for working. Perhaps we should start by defining motivation. A motivator is something which induces a person to act. Motivation can therefore be described as purposive behaviour directed towards achieving a goal. The goal may be physiological, for example, a thirsty individual will be motivated to find something to drink and their behaviour will be directed to that end. However other goals may be much more complex. In the early days of psychology attempts were made to list the basic human needs that motivate human behaviour. The lists became so long that the attempt was quietly abandoned!

In the previous chapter we examined Warr's view of what work has to offer the individual but the questions of why we choose to work at all, where we choose to work, and how much effort we expend whilst there, still need answering.

## The behaviourist model of motivation

**Behavioural** theory is based on the theories of **operant** and **classical conditioning** and is extended to **social learning theory**. It suggests that our behaviour is governed, or shaped, by the responses we meet in our environments. We will repeat behaviours which we find pleasant and which meet our needs, we will stop behaviours which produce no response and we will actually avoid unpleasant activities. This theory was highly influential in the early development of organisational psychology, particularly as it was taken up by Taylor (1911).

### Conditioning theory

#### Classical conditioning

Classical conditioning involves learning by association. If event A is consistently followed by event B then they will become associated. Event A will cause people and animals to anticipate event B. If you have a dog or cat and feed it on tinned food you will have observed that opening any tin produces a response from your pet. Your cat may wrap itself round your legs in an affectionate manner and your dog is likely to become excited. They have learned that open tins are often followed by food in their bowls.

Pavlov (1927) first described this after a number of observations he made in his laboratory experiments. Pavlov's dogs learned that food appeared soon after the researchers opened the laboratory door and the dogs began to salivate every time the door opened. He then created a series of experiments where a bell was rung every time that the dogs were fed. The dogs began to salivate in response to the sound of the bell, regardless of whether the food was present or not. Salivating in response to food is an unlearned (unconditioned) response. Salivating in response to a bell is a learned (conditioned) response. The dogs had been classically conditioned.

#### Operant conditioning

This is a more active explanation than classical conditioning and involves the individual acting or operating upon the environment. The individual engages in random activity, some of which may cause a response from the environment and some of which will have no effect. If no response is forthcoming the behaviour will not be repeated. However if the result of the action is rewarding to the individual then it is likely that they will repeat it.

Thorndike (1898) initially described this as instrumental learning and proposed a Law of Effect which stated that behaviour that is followed by a positive state of affairs (rewarded) is likely to be repeated. To put it another way, positive outcomes reinforce behaviour, failure to produce any outcome or providing a punishment discourages behaviour. Skinner (1938) developed this area of research much further and stated that all behaviour was manipulated by its consequences. In a typical experiment he placed hungry rats in a cage. If the animal pressed a lever in the cage then they would be provided with food. The rats soon incorporated lever pressing into their behaviour patterns and would press the lever when they became hungry. In other words they had learned that an action (pressing the lever) would produce a desired outcome (food) and the rat therefore quickly acquired (learned) the behaviour. In later experiments pressing the lever produced an electric shock and the rat stopped pressing the lever (at least in the short term) demonstrating that punishment made behaviour less likely to occur.

Let us apply this to a working situation. One of the rewards for working is receiving wages. If you are paid for working you are likely to go back again, your behaviour has been reinforced by a pleasurable outcome. If your behaviour produced no effect, i.e. you were not paid, it is unlikely that you would continue to work. If you were punished for going to work, perhaps by being treated in an extremely unpleasant way by your employer, maybe you would stop working for that company. Piece work, recommended by Taylor, is based on the notion that the worker is most highly motivated by finance and will therefore produce as many good quality pieces as possible in a given time because this is rewarding. Their wages are therefore based completely, or in part, on the number of good quality items they produce.

*Evaluation of conditioning theory*

One of the first problems which comes to mind is the establishment of rewards and punishments. It is easy to see that providing food to a hungry rat will be rewarding. When the question is applied to the complexities of everyday behaviour then the situation is not so simple. Docking someone's wages as a punishment for being late for work should, in theory, deter them from being late again. Being told off by a teacher for a similar offence should also produce the same effects. We all know that this is often not true. Rewards and punishments and their effects are unique to each individual. A further illustration of the dilemma occurs because the experience we gain at work may indeed be quite unpleasant but our wages for being there can put in place a wide range of rewards, varying from the means to survive to the holiday we have always dreamed of. Work can therefore both reward and punish at the same time and it is often extremely complex to work out an individual's behaviour using only the notion of reward and punishment as a guide. Life, as we shall see, is somewhat more complicated than a simple balance of reward and punishment.

It is important to ask what the individual thinks about the rewards and punishments. Do they want to learn the material or skills which are required? Having learned, do they want to produce the behaviour? Learning is one thing, doing what you have learned may be something completely different. A shop assistant may have received intensive training in being polite and obliging to customers. If they are faced with an extremely rude and aggressive shopper they may decide not to practise their well-learned skills. Also if we had to learn everything by reacting in a random way to our environment and acting on the consequences then life would be very tiresome! These thoughts led psychologists to suggest other ways in which people could learn and to propose that people actually thought out their actions, rather than being manipulated by their environments.

### Social learning theory

Albert Bandura (1974) developed Social Learning Theory. If you observe humans or animals you will have noticed that they often copy the behaviour of others rather than acting on the environment them-selves, particularly when they realise that the behaviour can produce a rewarding outcome. It makes sense to copy appropriate behaviour as it saves a great deal of time! Social learning occurs when an indi-vidual has the opportunity to model or copy behaviour by viewing an example. If the behaviour being watched is considered appropriate the individual may add it to their behavioural repertoire. This is even more likely to occur if the modelled behaviour is rewarded, referred to as vicarious reinforcement. Bandura (1974) stated that there were five stages to the process

1. pay attention to the model
2. record the behaviour, either as a visual image or as a semantic code by memorising instructions
3. store the memory of the performance efficiently
4. reproduce the actions of the model accurately
5. be motivated to reproduce the behaviour.

Bandura's model has been employed extensively in training for employment. Nurses learn to give injections by observing a nurse trainer, listening to him/her explaining their actions, practising the skills on an orange and receiving feedback before being allowed to use this treatment on patients. A golfer wishing to improve their swing will demonstrate their current performance to a more highly skilled player. This second player will analyse areas which need improvement, draw attention to faults and then demonstrate the new behaviour required to cause the improvement. The first player will then copy and practice the improved action, with the intention of improving their golf score. You will find a further example in Chapter 4 in the section on Training (pp. 58–59).

> Think of a skill which you have acquired recently. Using Bandura's stages describe how you became efficient and/or improved your performance.
>
> Review exercise

### Extrinsic and intrinsic motivation

So, you may ask, what is rewarding and what is not? We have already discussed the difficulties which exist in this area. Organisational psychologists have attempted to tackle the question of rewards by introducing the concepts of **extrinsic** and **intrinsic** motivation. Extrinsic rewards consist of external rewards which may be offered to the employee such as wages, holidays and material perks such as a company car. In general terms the presumption is that boring or dirty jobs present little that is intrinsically rewarding and that recruitment and workforce retention will therefore be governed by extrinsic factors. For example employees who work unsocial hours may be offered extra wages as it is presumed that they would not choose to do this work without some external or extrinsic reward. Intrinsic reward comes from internal feelings of satisfaction or pleasure which are found in carrying out the job. Skilled craftspeople will obtain this satisfaction from completing a well-produced piece of work. A talented artist may work to express their creativity rather than working for the price a painting might command. Education and Health Service workers are presumed to obtain intrinsic reinforcement from teaching and treating students and patients.

### Commentary on the behavioural approach

Behavioural principles have been used in employment situations. Rewards (incentives) and punishments (disincentives) are manipulated to affect behaviour in the workplace as we have just seen with the ideas of intrinsic and extrinsic motivation. Social learning theory's great impact has been on training and we will return to this issue in Chapter 4, however the approach sees human beings as automatons who can be manipulated by modifying their environments. During the 1960s and 1970s when behaviourism was felt to be an inadequate explanation of human activity, other approaches to motivation emerged.

## Maslow's hierarchy of needs

Perhaps the most important of the new approaches was Maslow's theory of motivation, the hierarchy of needs. Maslow was one of a group of psychologists who rejected the ideas of behaviourism, feeling that the behaviourists viewed human beings as machines and ignored their rich emotional and cognitive lives. His hierarchy of needs represents the **Humanist** approach to psychology. Maslow's work, first published in 1954, was one of the seminal works of the period and his approach became highly influential in organisational psychology and management training. Maslow proposed that humans have a basic hierarchy, or ascending scale of needs, which could be displayed as a pyramid or triangular structure (see Figure 3.1).

*Figure 3.1* **Maslow's hierarchy of needs**

*Physiological needs*

At the base of the pyramid are **physiological needs** such as food, drink, fresh air and shelter. Deprivation of a physiological need results in intensive activity to enable it to be met. For example, if an animal is hungry then it is motivated to hunt and forage to find food. Once the need has been met it ceases to be a motivator and the activity stops. If you are cold and wet then your activity will be directed to finding warmth and shelter. Other needs will be ignored. Maslow argued that the basic needs must be met before one could progress up the steps of the pyramid.

*Safety needs*

On the next step are **safety needs** by which Maslow meant a physical environment which is safe from extremes of weather and free from threats of attack by either human beings or animals. If shelter is not available individuals will work hard to obtain it. An environment where psychological threats are at a minimum is also a safety need. By this Maslow meant an environment which is predictable and one where the individual feels either in control or that those who are in control are benignly disposed towards them.

However once basic shelter has been obtained the individual will strive to improve their physical environment. They may, in fact, spend a good part of their 'leisure' time working to achieve such aims. Most of us would agree that the point at which an environment becomes safe and secure is highly subjective. A young person may be quite happy to share a house with others in a deprived inner-city area and may not be overly concerned about their own safety. A frail pensioner in the same circumstances may be terrified to leave their home and fearful of other residents in the building.

### Social needs

The third step up the pyramid is **social needs**. These come to the fore once physiological and safety needs are met. Most people live in and belong to a range of groups, such as families or the local neighbourhood. Work colleagues can form an important social group and relationships with our colleagues can be a source of pleasure. However, there are indications from Argyle (1988) that fellow workers, particularly superiors, can also be a source of conflict and unhappiness. There are also individuals, such as hermits, who prize social isolation. Maslow describes physiological, safety and social needs as *deficiency needs* on the grounds that we will put in a great deal of effort to obtain them and he believes that meeting them is a prerequisite for good psychological and physiological health.

### Esteem needs

The fourth step represents **esteem needs**, the desire for personal achievement and recognition by others. Perhaps this can be understood better as a need for self-respect and status. Maslow believed that this would not be our prime concern if the first three needs are not being met. If you return to the second step, it is apparent that there are individual variations in adequate provision of shelter. In our homes, we may concern ourselves with status as much as shelter.

Next come **growth needs** in that they represent activities which may not be essential but which occur in all human societies and which present the opportunity for personal growth and self-actualisation.

These include **cognitive needs**, the need to know, to understand and to explore our environment, ranging from the basic curiosity of a small child to the hard work involved in studying for a PhD, and **aesthetic needs**, the desire and need to appreciate beauty and symmetry. Maslow believed that this led to essentially human activities such as painting and writing poetry. Maslow felt that creative expression is intrinsically satisfying. Some people are able to meet these needs at work but for many of us they represent a valuable part of our leisure activities.

The fifth step or peak of the pyramid is **self-actualisation**, the feeling that the individual has truly fulfilled their potential. Maslow felt that this was a state which we should all aspire to but one which few of us would reach. Unlike the lower steps on the pyramid these needs become reinforcers in themselves. Fulfilling one's potential at this level is highly rewarding and the individual will always seek more self-actualisation.

### Commentary on Maslow's approach

The theory had tremendous impact when it was first published. Until then there had been a tendency to regard the labour force as one unit of expense and to ignore the emotional needs of the workers. This is perhaps best illustrated by a quote from a textbook published in 1973 which was introducing Maslow's theory and makes this comment about the impact it had upon management and organisational theory.

> More than the human relations movement it [Maslow's theory] has acted as a counterweight to the demands of the industrial engineer to deskill and simplify work, for it has resulted in attention being paid not only to the physical and social environment in which a job is done, but also to the actual content of the work itself, since it is only in a task that satisfaction of the higher level needs may be obtained at work.
>
> Drake and Smith 1973: 36

In other words higher level needs could be met in the workplace. Workers were fellow human beings and not just units of production. Intrinsic motivation and the fulfilment of growth needs were essential in motivating employees.

Maslow's work represents an optimistic view of human nature. However it has recently been open to criticism. For example people composed poetry in the concentration camps. Fasting has been used in many cultures as a tool to improve self-knowledge. Other individuals have chosen to starve for a strongly held political belief. People can be motivated by higher needs when lower ones are not being satisfied or they can choose the higher need before the lower one. How does this fit in to the hierarchy?

In spite of these comments it is still the first four needs, physiological, safety, social and esteem needs, which are presumed to be met, either directly or indirectly, in the workplace. Wages, the environment in which we work, our contacts with our fellows and our status in the organisation are most likely to be manipulated to make us work harder, i.e. to motivate us to perform better. An illustration of the difficulty in applying Maslow's theory can be seen in the controversy over the salaries offered to sports personalities. Which is the greater motivator for a professional footballer: £50,000 per week or an international cap?

The theory was very much a product of its time and is very western in its basic tenets. Maslow interprets social and esteem needs in an individualistic way. As already indicated, the point at which any individual's needs become satisfied is highly subjective. Is self-actualisation applicable in the workplace at all? It is not clear exactly what it is and it is impossible to test. In reality it must be very difficult to satisfy many higher needs when employed in a basic, boring task on a production line! This is not necessarily a fault but it makes it an extremely difficult concept to apply effectively in organisational settings.

Progress exercise

There is controversy in the UK about the so-called 'benefits trap'. Why do we expect people to work if their wages are the same or less than state benefits? What would their motivation be?

## McClelland: the need for achievement

Whilst Maslow feels that our ultimate aim or motivator is self-actualisation, McClelland (1985) suggested that we work to fulfil internal needs, including a need for achievement (**nAch**). McClelland developed his theory specifically with the workplace in mind. His study was based on interviews with businessmen and government administrators in the USA, Italy, Poland and Turkey, adolescent boys in Brazil, India and Japan, and villagers in India and Japan. He also looked at government documents and cultural artefacts. He concluded that people's motivation at work fell into three main areas.

1. *The need for achievement* is a basic desire to succeed and to get a task completed as effectively as possible. Individuals with a high need for achievement will always strive for excellence and will enjoy working to achieve their goal. They view problem solving as a positive challenge and take great pride in their achievements.
2. *The need for power* is the desire for high status. Individuals with a high need for power like to control their own and others' working environments. This is more important to them than, for example, problem solving.
3. *The need for affiliation* is concerned with relationships at work and the need to be accepted as group members. It involves co-operation rather than competition and getting on with workmates is more important than being promoted.

All workers have these three needs or requirements but McClelland believed that one need is more dominant than the others in each individual. For example he believed that successful managers need to have high power and achievement needs but low affiliation needs. Whereas workers would have lower needs for achievement but higher affiliation needs. If an employer can successfully match an individual's needs to their job then a high rate of performance and productivity can be expected.

The need for achievement (nAch) is the most widely discussed and researched of these three needs and this idea has been highly influential in both work structuring and selection of employees. McClelland (1965) completed a longtitudinal study following the progress of men who had been rated as having high or low nAch. Eighty three per cent of those with high nAch scores obtained high-status posts, compared to 21 per cent of the low scorers. Koestner and McClelland (1990) suggest that societies with a high nAch have higher levels of productivity than those with a low nAch.

People with a high nAch are said to

- set achievable goals for themselves
- seek to master tasks and gain intense satisfaction from their achievements
- consistently strive for improvement
- have a strong sense of initiative
- enjoy assuming personal responsibility for the task in hand
- value both personal and organisational growth.

These qualities, all of which involve intrinsic motivation, are highly prized and it will not come as a surprise to know that many successful sporting personalities are said to display a high nAch. Successful football managers are those who create a high need to win in their players. Atkinson (1974) has developed a model, using nAch to improve sports performance and there is a well-known saying in the USA 'show me a good loser and I'll show you a loser'.

### Commentary on McClelland's approach

McClelland believed that these characteristics are learned in early childhood, particularly by young males from their fathers. McClelland (1985) discovered that parents of nAch children actively encouraged their children to take up difficult tasks and praised them when they succeeded. If the child did not succeed they were encouraged to try alternative strategies and discouraged from giving up. Once the task was completed they were encouraged to move on to a more difficult one. Most of his interviewees were male. Dweck (1986), who has produced a number of studies in the USA, by observing and questioning school age children about their educational achievements, has indicated that there are differences between males and females in nAch. Boys and girls may be socialised differently and the need to achieve and be successful in employment may be emphasised to boys while the role of carer is emphasised to girls. Dweck noted that girls did not always set challenging goals and were less likely to persist if they were anxious about possible failure. Girls were also more likely to see failure as a result of their own low ability. This may be because they also received different feedback to boys, indicating that their ability was at fault if they do not do well. Boys were encouraged to try harder and their effort rather than their ability was blamed for poor performance. It may be that McClelland has interpreted male behaviour as universal and has ignored female approaches to work.

Despite the cross-cultural range of McClelland's sample there are also indications that different cultures interpret achievement in different ways. In countries where the kin group or the community's needs are seen to be of more significance than those of the individual, the reasons for success and failure may be attributed differently, as less emphasis is placed upon the individual's contribution. In an article published by Zahrani and Kaplowitz (1993) participants from the USA and Saudi Arabia were asked about a number of short stories concerned with successful task accomplishment. Those from the USA attributed success to the individual whilst those from Saudi Arabia attributed it to the help which individuals received from others. This research confirms previous statements that theories in organisational psychology are culture bound because they view organisational patterns which have developed in the west as the norm and ignore those found in other societies. They are also gender-bound as they ignore the experience of women. When transferred into working practices the implications become clearer. Promotion in most western companies and organisations is often based on the individual's personal achievements. Women and those from ethnic minorities may be less willing to put themselves forward for challenging tasks. If they do produce an outstanding piece of work they may attribute their success to the assistance of others in their team or to good luck.

1. Give two examples of patterns of work in western organisations which may lead managers to assume that some groups do not have a high nAch.

2. Indicate which groups might be affected and explain how this occurs.

Progress exercise

## Job satisfaction

If work is meeting needs one must raise the issue of job satisfaction. Do individuals work to obtain money to meet basic needs for food and shelter or does work offer other rewards? It may be appropriate to examine two theories concerned with satisfaction at work.

### Behavioural theory

Behavioural theory suggests that work is satisfying in so far as it provides positive reinforcement. This would suggest that bonuses, piece work or performance-related pay would be effective strategies for getting people to work harder. The idea being that the greater the financial reward the more satisfying the job will be. As we have already suggested things are not so clear cut because pay is not the only motivator in the workplace. Individuals may also work harder for personal satisfaction, to recieve positive feedback from colleagues or superiors or to obtain status.

## Herzberg's two-factor theory

Herzberg (1966) believed that previous researchers had confused job satisfaction and job dissatisfaction and suggested that work involves two sets of needs: **hygiene needs** and **motivator needs**.

Hygiene needs relate to environmental factors and are met by the physical and psychological conditions in the workplace including salary, job security, working conditions, co-workers and the management structure. Dissatisfaction will occur if these conditions are not met. For example we would not be happy working in a dirty, unsafe workplace for poor wages. This infers that an employer who creates a congenial and safe environment and pays his workers well should reduce dissatisfaction and have happier and harder-working employees.

Motivator needs are attached to the task itself. These would be responsibility, opportunities for personal growth, credit for tasks accomplished, potential for promotion and the responsibilities one is given. The fulfilment of these needs should lead to increased job satisfaction and Herzberg presumes that people will work harder to gain more satisfaction. High job satisfaction would occur when all or most of these needs are being met. One can see the overlap here between hygiene needs and extrinsic motivators and motivator needs and intrinsic motivators. A high salary may provide satisfaction that offsets a boring job which has low esteem from others.

## Commentary on Herzberg's approach

Herzberg's work was based on interviews with a small sample of male engineers and accountants and it is difficult to generalise to construct a theory which fits workforces in all parts of the world. Landy (1985) suggests that the two-factor theory represents the way people think of satisfaction at work in western settings but it is not open to proof. The results may be an example of the **fundamental attribution error**. This states that we attribute our successes to internal factors, such as our use of skills or ability to work hard (motivator needs) and our failures to external factors, such as the conditions in which we work or the attitude of others (hygiene needs).

Katz (1978) suggested that job satisfaction might not stay constant throughout working life. He interviewed 3,085 employees working in the public sector for government agencies and in the private sector in industry in the USA. He examined the relationship between job satisfaction and the length of time in employment and discovered that it changed over time. New employees enjoyed the task itself and appreciated positive feedback from fellow workers. After 6 months they became confident in their performance and satisfaction was obtained from increasing autonomy, in particular they enjoyed being responsible for the whole task and using a variety of skills. The longer they stayed with their employers the less the actual task mattered. One presumes that the task loses its challenge and the individual takes their own proficiency for granted. By the time an individual has been in a post for 15 years pay and benefits become important, together with relationships with management and colleagues. This suggests that job satisfaction is far more complex than Herzberg suggests.

There are also suggestions that workers may create their own satisfaction when the task is extremely boring and unsatisfying. Roy (1960) completed a participant observation in a factory where the work was routine and boring. Workers created their own satisfaction from personal interaction. A lot of time was spent in horseplay and silly behaviour; for example one man stole his workmate's lunchtime banana every day. Burawoy repeated the study in 1979 and found the situation virtually unchanged. If you chat to people working on building sites you will elicit similar stories. Apparently the TV series *Aufwiedersehen Pet* presented an underestimate of the level of this kind of activity.

**Review exercise**

Make a list of the six factors which you believe to be the most important in motivating people to work. Explain how you would implement two of these in the workplace.

## Summary

This chapter has introduced the topic of motivation for work. It began by exploring the potential rewards for working and the concepts of intrinsic or internal satisfaction and extrinsic or externally provided incentives. We then went on to consider two theories of motivation which are popular in organisational psychology. First, Maslow's hierarchy of needs, a humanistic approach to motivation which states that humans have a basic desire to move towards growth and self-actualisation but can only do so when basic needs are met. Second, McClelland looked at needs in a working environment and stated that humans have three basic needs at work, including the need to achieve (nAch) which marks out those who will be highly successful. It was noted that both these ideas are a product of western culture. The topic of job satisfaction was then introduced and Herzberg's two-factor theory of hygiene and motivator needs discussed. Hygiene needs are similar to extrinsic needs and motivator needs to extrinsic ones. Research by Katz and the Banana study by Roy were also described and linked with Herzberg's theory.

## Further reading

Maslow, A.H. (1970) *Motivation and Personality* 2nd edn., New York: Harper Row. It is best to return to the original text. Maslow's work has suffered from some amazing interpretations since it was published! Although some of the ideas may appear outdated it is a useful, seminal text.

McClelland, D.C. (1984) *Human Motivation*, Cambridge: Cambridge University Press. This is one of the most influential texts in organisational psychology. It examines the links between economic development, cultural expectations and motivation. Although the research concerned itself mainly with boys, it displayed a link between socialisation processes in childhood and adult attitudes to work. The text is aimed at managers rather than students.

# Selection and training

## Introduction

Recruitment and training were among the first branches of **industrial psychology** that used the services of psychologists. The process of recruiting workers can be expensive and it becomes increasingly costly if the workers fail to perform competently or if they leave prematurely. Similarly the applicant is hoping to find a job which they will enjoy and which will offer a fair rate of pay. The process of selection should benefit both parties if it is well done.

Most of you will be familiar with the process of selection for either a full- or part-time job and many of you will have received careers guidance and will therefore have some knowledge of this area. Therefore you are probably aware of the many external constraints that impinge on the procedure, such as the local level of employment and unemployment. Also the criteria a student will use in seeking part-time employment will probably differ from those they will use when choosing a career after leaving full-time education. One could therefore use the old truism and say that the purpose of selection is to avoid putting square pegs in round holes, particularly if either party intends to invest heavily in the long-term outcome of the process.

### Personnel and human resources departments

The **personnel** or **human resources** section is the department in a company with the specific responsibility of staffing. It is usual for this department to administer selection procedures and to deal with staff welfare and it is an area where organisational psychologists have been heavily involved. In some organisations this department is also responsible for training.

## Selection for employment

### Job analysis

One technique used by employers to describe a job is **job analysis**. This leads to a **job specification** so that the employer can define the type of skills and characteristics needed, and the potential employee has an indication of exactly what the job will entail. This should act as an initial filter for both parties.

There are various methods used to analyse tasks and draw up a job specification. The usual practice involves a combination of methods. The first, and perhaps most obvious, is to observe the actual job whilst it is being done. To avoid errors a number of workers should be observed. The next step would involve interviewing people who do the job and also others who work with them, including colleagues and line managers. Finally existing literature should be examined, including previous specifications and those for broadly similar jobs. This job specification should enable the employer to draw up a **person specification**. Furnham (1997) suggests that a job analysis should provide details of

- the minimum professional knowledge that would be acceptable
- the range of basic skills required
- the ideal personality traits that the job holder should have.

These three items are frequently referred to as *knowledge, skills and attitudes*.

### Describing the job

The next stage would be to advertise the post giving details of the knowledge, skills and attitudes required, working conditions and potential remuneration. Provided that the job appears attractive enough to encourage sufficient people to apply, the employer then has to initiate some form of selection to ensure that they employ the most suitable worker.

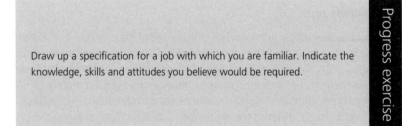

Draw up a specification for a job with which you are familiar. Indicate the knowledge, skills and attitudes you believe would be required.

Progress exercise

As yet there is no foolproof method of selection for employment and the methods chosen are likely to reflect the needs of the organisation and the resources that are available. Many of the readers of this book will be applying for a place at university or a job using an application form containing a personal statement (biodata), a reference from the educational establishment they attend (attitudes and personality), and their predicted grades (knowledge and skills). The majority of university applicants will not be interviewed unless they are applying for an occupation such as nursing, where personality and self-presentation are thought to be important, or they are applying for a highly prestigious course. Those who move into employment will almost certainly be asked to attend for a personal interview. You may like to spend some time considering the reasons for this difference.

Progress exercise

Give two reasons why employers are likely to use personal interviews and most higher education establishments do not.

You may wish to consider the relative costs involved and the numbers of applicants who may be involved.

## Knowledge, skills and attitudes

### *Work sample tests*

It does not take a great deal of psychological knowledge or common sense to realise that knowledge and skills are much easier to measure than attitudes. Knowledge and skills lend themselves to objective assessment. For example either someone can type accurately at 60 words per minute or they can not, however an individual can effectively disguise their attitudes for the period of an interview or assessment.

Knowledge can be checked by asking for appropriate qualifications or by giving tests. An applicant for a job which involves accurate handling of figures can be given a maths test. Skills can be measured in the same way. The applicant can be asked to provide a work sample. A clerical worker could be asked to do some filing or a teacher may be asked to do an observed 30-minute class. Both of these techniques have high **face** and **predictive validity**. By face validity we mean that the individual is performing a task which is accurately representing the job they will have to do. On the face of it the two tasks look the same. Predictive validity indicates that the job sample will give an accurate forecast of the way the candidate will perform if they are appointed. However work samples are by nature highly test specific, being limited to the task undertaken and do not give indications of flexibility and adaptation to new situations. This means that you can test someone in one situation and infer that they have a range of similar skills which they can use in different environments. In fact they may not be able to transfer their skills.

### Psychometric testing and assessment

The search for effective testing techniques to choose good employees with the appropriate knowledge, skills and attitudes and predict future success is something like the search for the Holy Grail. It would be wonderful if such materials existed and a great deal of time and energy has been spent in searching for them. Let us look at some of the tests and techniques which are used.

*Intelligence tests*

**Intelligence tests** may be used to attempt to assess an individual's underlying ability to problem solve and adapt effectively to their environment. These tests were initially developed as a selection tool in educational settings at the beginning of the twentieth century but were rapidly adopted for the same purpose in other situations.

An individual completes a test or series of tests and the score should indicate their level of intellectual competence, as measured by that particular test. Tests may be completed in groups or on a one-to-one basis. A one-to-one test can take up to 2 hours to complete. A popular example is the tests designed by Wechsler in the USA (Wechsler 1955). The adult form being the WAIS (Wechsler Adult Intelligence Test). This consists of a batch of tests which assess verbal abilities such as vocabulary, general knowledge, comprehension and maths and non-verbal or performance skills such as copying patterns with blocks and picture completion. The tester may ask the individual about decisions on some items and will provide a comprehensive report. Block tests can be given to groups and are marked later, often by someone who did not administer the test. This means that the tester has no idea why particular answers are given. A typical example of a block test is Ravens Progressive Matrices which aims to assess problem-solving skills and the ability to see spatial relationships. The individual is presented with a series of visual puzzles which become progressively more difficult. There are several sets of pictures and the exercise is timed.

COMMENTARY ON THE USE OF INTELLIGENCE TESTS

In employment selection the usual procedure is to use group tests which are cheap and easy to administer, however, these tend to be less accurate than one-to-one testing. Whilst they may be more widely applicable than work sampling they still lack predictive validity for many jobs. Because many of the tests were developed for educational settings , they measure academic ability and this may not be related to job performance. Porteous (1997) points out a university degree and a good job can both be obtained by individuals who do not score very highly on intelligence tests, whilst some individuals who score very highly on such tests may appear to be dull because they lack basic social skills and may perform very poorly in the workplace. The tests have been criticised for being culture specific as the general knowledge questions are often culture bound. If, in a block test, only one answer can be marked as accurate what happens if there are ambiguities. A wrong answer may be perfectly logical to the person being tested. For example if you were asked to find the odd one out in this list: grapefruit, lemon, banana and orange, is it banana because it is not a citrus fruit or is it the orange because all the others are yellow. Those who use the tests claim that such problems are eliminated when the tests are being designed.

Other tests, such as the Ravens Progressive Matrices (Raven 1965) mentioned above, attempt to measure a less culture-bound range of abilities such as spatial skills, the ability to deal with the relationships of objects to each other in terms of depth and movement, and the ability to perform skills such as map reading. However they are still often used on groups of individuals who are very different to those the tests were designed for. For example Ravens Matrices is logical for those who are used to these kinds of problem-solving exercises from school, or the use of puzzle books at home, but it may appear to be a totally pointless exercise to someone who did not share this cultural back-ground. There is also the problem of **test sophistication**, meaning that the more tests of a particular kind that a person does the faster their performance becomes. If the individual is scored by timing then a confounding variable will occur as their high score will be due to the effects of practice as well as their ability in that test. However Ghiselli (1966) demonstrated that intelligence tests were good predictors of performance for executives and administrators.

Progress exercise

List the strengths and weaknesses of the use of individual and group intelligence tests in a work setting. Look at the economic issues involved and balance time against usefulness.

*Testing or measuring attitudes*

In any job an individual's social skills will impinge on their work performance, as they will probably have to work as part of a team and be responsible to or for others. It does not matter how well an individual performs if they irritate or antagonise their co-workers or customers. Employers are also looking for characteristics such as punctuality, honesty, reliability and effective use of skills. Ability tests and work sampling cannot give effective indications of these. This leads to the use of other techniques the simplest of which is to ask for references from previous employers or from others who know the individual. However it is possible that references are misleading. Employers have been known to deliberately write flattering references, which are often economical with the truth, if they wish to get rid of an individual. I personally recall receiving a reference for a female employee stating 'she frequently bends over backwards to show herself in a good light'. It was not long before the organisation realised that this was not referring to her helpful personality!

This leaves the thorny area of attitudes. These are notoriously difficult to assess. One technique used by vocational courses, such as training for social work, is to place applicants in a group and ask them to discuss a pertinent subject. The interviewers will attempt to assess attitudes by responses made to the subject matter.

Another technique is the use of **projective tests**, such as the thematic apperception test (TAT). This test consists of twenty pictures and drawings of two or more individuals in a range of ambiguous social settings. The person completing the test is asked to make up a story to explain what is happening. The stories are analysed by the tester to see what 'themes' appear. The interpretation of these themes will give clues to the individual's unconscious mind and predictions can be made about their attitudes.

## COMMENTARY ON PROJECTIVE TESTS

Projective tests are highly subjective and rely heavily on the skill of the tester. Their subjectivity leads to problems of **reliability**. A test is reliable if it produces consistent results. Projective tests were developed in **clinical** settings where the staff using them were highly trained in the use of similar methods of interpretation. In work settings individuals using tests may not be trained to such a high standard. Two different individuals who are not well trained in interpreting projective tests would be likely to produce highly inconsistent results. This is an area we will return to when considering **personality tests**.

### Personality tests

Blinkhorn and Johnson (1990) estimated that half the companies in the UK use personality tests in their selection procedures. Eysenck (1998) stated that **intelligence testing** (see pp. 45–47) represents an area that has 'generated more heat than light', meaning that such tests create more ripples than they do information. Personality tests create even greater controversy.

Personality tests aim to give employers and others a picture of an individual's basic characteristics so that these can be matched against the demands of the job. They are based on the notion of stable underlying characteristics, which can be measured, usually, by answering a batch of questions. There are a large number of tests available, some of which are general and some of which are specific for certain occupations. Two of the best known tests are Eysenck's personality inventory and Cattell's dimensions of personality (Cattell 1965).

## EYSENCK'S PERSONALITY INVENTORY

Eysenck's personality test has been in existence for over 30 years and is based on the concept of different personality types, namely **extroverts** and **introverts**. Extroverts are said to be sociable, outgoing and lively. They are impulsive, like taking risks and are difficult to condition. They have a low level of anxiety and it is difficult to use the processes of operant and classical conditioning to enable them to learn. Introverts are quiet, conscientious and often enjoy their own company. They tend to be cautious, have a high level of anxiety and are easy to condition. Eysenck's test also measures personality against the level of psychoticism and on a neurotic/tough-minded axis. Those scoring high for psychoticism are likely to be loners who are aggressive, hostile and insensitive to others' feelings. The test is based on the belief that these are underlying biological characteristics and will therefore be consistent and can be used to predict behaviour. Eysenck's personality inventory has been used extensively in clinical and academic research. The fact that it has been helpful in these assessments is one confirmation of the validity of the test.

Eysenck's personality inventory is also used in occupational settings. The individual is assessed by completing a series of questions which require Yes/No answers. The test includes a **lie scale** to try to exclude the answers of those who are using the test to give a favourable impression rather than answering honestly. The results can be used to attempt to match individuals to jobs. The underlying assumption is particular jobs require particular personality types.

## CATTELL'S 16 FACTOR TEST

Cattell's test, which also has a 30-year history, is based on the idea of sixteen **source traits** which can vary in the individual. For example there are traits such as dominant/submissive, conformist/unconventional and radical/conservative (see Figure 4.1) The characteristics were developed after extensive research in the USA that attempted to list basic characteristics or source traits. As with Eysenck the underlying assumption is that these traits are stable and can therefore be used to predict behaviour. An individual answers a questionnaire which allows three choices, Yes/Occasionally/No, and a personality profile is constructed from the responses.

## Commentary on psychometric tests

Personality testing causes even greater controversy than intelligence testing. There is a variety of psychological opinion in this area. At one extreme some psychologists will reject the use of these tests completely, claiming that they lack both validity and reliability, and are a waste of

---

### Cattell's 16 personality factors

1. Reserved/outgoing
2. Less intelligent/more intelligent
3. Affected by feelings/emotionally stable
4. Humble/assertive
5. Sober/happy-go-lucky
6. Expedient/conscientious
7. Shy/venturesome
8. Tough minded/tender minded
9. Trusting/suspicious
10. Practical/imaginative
11. Straightforward/shrewd
12. Self assured/apprehensive
13. Conservative/experimenting
14. Group dependent/self-sufficient
15. Self-conflict/self-control
16. Relaxed/tense

---

*Figure 4.1* Cattell's personality traits

valuable time and resources. At the other extreme you will find psychologists who believe that the tests are an essential guide in employment selection and that employers who ignore these assets are wasting valuable time and resources. As ever, the truth lies somewhere in the middle ground.

Critics of personality tests claim that the tests lack validity and reliability because it is easy to cheat. Intelligent candidates will give the answers that they feel are appropriate, rather than telling the truth. The tests are therefore not measuring the individual's personality but are eliciting the responses which the candidate feels the employer requires for that job. The test results will therefore also not be consistent. If a test is well designed and includes a lie scale, those who design and support the tests believe that this kind of cheating can be detected. For example a statement such as 'I have never been late in my life' would be seen as so improbable that it would rate as a lie.

There is also a problem with the underlying assumption of stable personality characteristics. Many psychologists claim that personality will vary in differing environments and will change and develop as an individual responds to life experiences. Supporters of tests claim that particular personality types and characteristics associate with particular areas of employment. For example there is evidence that successful salespeople score highly on tests for extroversion. The problem here is the question of whether successful salespeople are extroverts or whether a period in such employment causes extrovert characteristics to develop. Jessup and Jessup (1971) correlated scores on Eysenck's personality inventory and success in pilot training in the Royal Air Force. Those with low neuroticism and low extraversion scores were most likely to succeed in the tests. However personality inventories completed by successful practising pilots show a different picture. They still produce low scores for neuroticism but score highly for extraversion. This either indicates that training and practice each need different personality types or confirms that the social situation comes to affect performance on tests. It is likely that an individual's behaviour will change over time as they learn from experience. Their reactions may differ with the situation in which they find themselves but whether these can be measured or quantified objectively forms the heart of the controversy in their use.

The problem is compounded by the fact that some employers buy tests, such as Eysenck's personality inventory or Cattell's 16 factor test, and then interpret the results themselves. As the interpretation of the tests relies on a psychologist or someone with expert training this undermines the validity of the tests further.

*Ethical issues in psychometric testing*

There are ethical issues with both personality and intelligence tests. If the completed tests are filed who will be able to access the results? Will confidentiality be assured? How long will the results be stored? The results of tests date quickly and it would not be appropriate to use them several years later. If someone completes a batch of tests when they first enter a company would the results be either useful or appropriate 10 years later? How should material of this nature be used? If the tests are completed for one post in a company and the individual moves to a different task in another section of the company should the new line manager have access to the previous results?

## Biodata

**Biodata** takes a different approach. Goldsmith first used the system in 1922. It involves interviewing and observing individuals who are already in post and listing the environmental factors which are commonly found in

- successful long-term employees
- employees who have been unsatisfactory or who have left after a very short time.

Application forms, known as **weighted application blanks** are then constructed to elicit standard items of biographical information, which have been commonly found in previous successful employees. Alternatively **curriculum vitae** are examined and matched against the selected criteria.

The procedure is similar to that used in risk assessment for life or motor insurance. Premiums for motor insurance are based on the probability that certain individuals will make more claims than other individuals. Premiums are increased for those considered to be a high risk or insurance might be refused completely. Individuals are described in terms of their **demographic details** such as age, sex, marital status, home location, education and health. In terms of job applications up to twenty factors could be considered including hobbies. The presumption is that an employer has details of what kind of person will best fit the particular job. This 'profile' can then be used to predict who will be successful in a post in the future. This approach has proved popular in the past and is often used on an informal basis.

### Commentary on the biodata approach

This approach may not prove as successful in an environment where job specifications continuously change. Perhaps the most important criticism is that this approach is highly discriminatory. If men have traditionally done a job such an approach would not indicate the possibility of employing women, on the basis that you do not change a system which is successful. It could also discriminate against immigrant groups if criteria such as a history of residence in a particular area are used and it would not credit unfamiliar and newer qualifications. In the long term it could lead to a stale approach and the company becoming out of date. If the approach is used it must therefore be updated every few years.

## Interviews

Presuming that the applicants have survived filling in an application form, completing psychometric tests and other initial methods of selection, it is likely that those who appear to have the best fit for the job will be invited for interview. Interviews may take a structured or unstructured approach.

### Unstructured interviews

**Unstructured interviews** are similar to an informal chat. The employer does not have a set series of questions to ask, there may not be a time limit and the procedure might vary enormously from one candidate to the next. Porteous (1997) believes that these interviews frequently turn into conversations about holidays or sport. Not surprisingly such a hit-and-miss approach has hit-and-miss results. Herriot (1989) states that they are prone to sex bias as the interviewers are often male and are more likely to digress into comfortable chats with someone who has similar interests.

### Structured interviews

Most employers, therefore, use a **structured interview** where set questions are asked in a particular order of all candidates (a sort of verbal psychometric testing exercise). Questions will usually cover the candidate's knowledge required for the job, the candidate's response to commonly experienced working situations, and the candidate's willingness and ability to fit in with the specific demands of the company.

### Commentary on the use of interviews for selection

The most obvious advantage is that the interview is a social encounter and it offers the first face-to-face contact between the applicant and potential employer. It offers each individual an initial impression of each other and allows withdrawal or rejection if there is an obvious mismatch. However interviewers have to make important judgements and a small sample of behaviour is used to make long-term predictions. As interviewing is such a commonly used selection tool it has generated a great deal of research. Mayfield (1964) completed a **meta analysis** where he gathered together and analysed data from eighty research studies, he concluded that success at an interview was not useful in predicting success upon appointment.

## Attribution theory

During interviews the effects of **attribution theory** are evident. Attribution theory refers to the tendency of an individual to use impressions to make judgements about a person's characteristics and personality on the basis of insufficient information. We need to make sense of the world and often take short cuts when making judgements about the personalities of others. It has been said that success or failure in an interview is determined in the first few seconds. Psychologists use the term **primacy effects** to describe the fact that first impressions often influence our beliefs about a person more than subsequent impressions. There is also evidence of the **fundamental attribution error**. This is the tendency to explain other people's behaviour in terms of their personality or disposition, rather than a consequence of the social situation they are in. Judgements made in interview situations are often made about individual characteristics from behaviour which may well be a product of the situation rather than aspects of the individual's personality. Herriot (1981) has demonstrated these effects in graduate-selection interviews. He noted that any unusual aspect in a candidate's behaviour at interview or which occurred on their application form or curriculum vitae caused a range of characteristics to be attributed to them, however, this did not occur when application forms and CVs did not contain such information. Arvey (1979), who has investigated discriminatory behaviour in selection procedures, has indicated that the more dissimilar the interviewer and the applicant are, then the more unsuccessful the interview will be. He stated that unfavourable racial and gender **stereotypes** can come into play and that an interviewer will attribute positive characteristics to applicants who are like them and negative ones to those who are different. This research demonstrated that women interviewed by men were given poorer evaluations than men were, even if they had equivalent qualifications. This was particularly true for senior or managerial posts where there was a previous history and expectation that males would fill these jobs. It is likely that the same effects occur in interviews with minority groups. You may have heard this referred to as the 'glass ceiling', meaning that there is an invisible barrier to some higher paid jobs because of an attribution that women or people from ethnic minorities cannot do them. Basically the argument is that since no one of this description has been observed doing the job then they must belong to a group incapable of doing so.

### *Forming an impression*

There is consistent evidence that non-verbal criteria such as dress, eye contact and general demeanour are used, even if they are not formally acknowledged. Dipboye and Wiley (1977) asked recruiters to interview two candidates with very similar experience and qualifications. Each candidate presented differently at interview. Candidate one was described as passive, they spoke softly and failed to maintain eye contact. When asked questions they appeared underconfident, often gave one-word answers or prefixed their responses with 'I think' or 'I guess'. They failed to respond to the interviewer's attempts to help them participate more actively in the interview. Applicant two behaved assertively and engaged actively in the interview. They smiled, used eye contact effectively and responded confidently and in detail to the interviewer's questions. Not only was applicant two more likely to be invited for a second interview but their experience and qualifications were rated as superior to candidate one, even though this was not the case.

Over the past 20 years a highly negative stereotype has emerged of overweight people who are likely to be described as lazy, greedy and undesirable. There is increasing evidence that this stereotype affects their employment options. When photographs of fat and thin hands filling in application forms were shown to people, they viewed the applications from the fat hands less favourably (Larkin and Pines 1979). Benson *et al.* (1980) attached photographs of fat and thin candidates to identical curriculum vitae. The fat candidates were less likely to be called for interview and also less likely to be appointed. There are indications that women are particularly badly affected by this kind of stereotyping.

Despite these limitations the interview is the most commonly used selection technique and is as successful as other methods. As previously stated it allows the interviewer and interviewee the chance to meet which, at the very least, prevents 'hate at first site' when the applicant starts the job. It also allows doubts and problems to be aired.

**Progress exercise**

1. Choose two different jobs and select the appropriate methods to use to assess the suitability of candidates who apply for these jobs.

2. How much and what kind of information do you need? Which factors would you try to avoid in the selection process?

## Training

Once employees are in post it is likely that they will be offered induction and training to enable them to function effectively. They may also be offered further training once in post to prepare them for changes in employment patterns or for internal promotion or movement. This again represents an expense for employers and may be done in house 'on the job', that is on the employer's premises, or 'off the job' by sending the employee to a college or training organisation. The process of selecting employees for training is one of the areas in which human resources departments and occupational psychologists are most frequently involved. The role of occupational psychologists would be to design and choose the most appropriate methods to enable the employee to succeed at the minimum cost to the employer. These two demands may be in conflict.

### Training needs analysis

In order for training to be effective it must be well organised and planned. If it is done on an *ad hoc* basis or purely to meet short-term emergency situations it is likely to be ineffective and costly. It is therefore usual to make a **training needs analysis** consisting of

• organisational analysis

- task analysis
- person analysis.

*Organisational analysis*

This involves asking the organisation to specify its present and future goals. It is then necessary to examine the organisation and identify the best way to achieve these goals and the barriers which may be in the way. An example of this could be the introduction of new equipment, such as replacing typewriters with word processors. Another may be discontinuing inefficient working practices and/or introducing new working methods. The cost of making existing staff redundant and employing new workers will be balanced against the cost of retraining existing staff. The organisation will then have to assess and cost the training needs of existing and new staff and balance this against the cost of redundancies.

*Task analysis*

This entails compiling the following information about the task/s to be completed

- the skills needed by the practitioner
- the materials required
- the tools and equipment required to complete the task
- the time to complete the job to a satisfactory standard
- the optimum physical environment and the services required in that environment
- the cost of the training.

Different individuals within the organisation may prioritise these elements in different orders. Often the task analysis reflects priorities within the company. Human resources departments may prioritise item one whilst the company accountant may insist that the last item takes priority.

*Person analysis/personal appraisal*

This involves matching the individual to the needs of the job and appraising, or assessing, their performance at regular intervals. With the often changing demands of the modern workplace this process is continuous in most organisations. The process usually consists of a personal interview with the worker, asking them about their current performance and future plans, giving them feedback on these topics, assessing their existing skills and comparing them with the skills that they will need to complete their present and future tasks. An action plan should then be produced in which both assessor and employee agree on long-term goals. Unfortunately performance appraisals tend to be highly subjective and subject to biases such as rating similar qualities to those of the appraiser more highly than others, being influenced by the person's physical appearance or being most influenced by their most recent behaviour rather than looking over the whole period of appraisal. Obviously service industries, where actual outcomes are notoriously difficult to measure, is most open to this kind of bias. None the less good training needs analysis and effective personal appraisal will not only identify training and development needs but also the most appropriate strategy for delivering the training.

### Using the principles of learning theory

Most training uses the principles of social learning theory rather than classical or operant conditioning learning theory, and applies these to specific situations. For example a skill would be demonstrated to the learner, who would then be given the opportunity to practise the skill in a supervised setting until it becomes automatic, i.e. it can be completed without conscious thought and without supervision. The same technique can be used with managerial tasks. Latham and Saari (1979) used observational training with a group of foremen. A control group in the same organisation received no training. The foremen received input on topics important to supervisors such as motivation and introducing new working techniques. Films of individuals modelling these techniques were shown, accompanied by indications from the trainer where the behaviour was appropriate. The foremen then role played these behaviours and received praise (positive reinforcement) for appropriate behaviour. The group who received training were assessed and observed and were rated as performing significantly better than the controls. If you refer back to Chapter 3 you will see that this programme follows Bandura's recommendations (p. 26–27) The foremen had to observe behaviour, memorise it and then practise it.

### *Transfer of training*

If an individual is being retrained or their skills are being upgraded the question of **transfer of training** arises. Transfer may be positive and the individual may build on existing skills. For example, someone who has ridden a pushbike can transfer many of the skills to riding a motor bike. A further example is pilots who learn the skills of flying an aeroplane in a simulator before flying the real thing. However it may be negative when older skills conflict with the newer ones and make the new learning extremely difficult. You may have experienced this when you or a member of your family has taken a motoring holiday in Europe. The skill of driving is very well practised and therefore done without conscious thought. When faced with driving on the opposite side of the road most people find the task extremely difficult and find their old habits taking over. Conversations on the first few miles after disembarking from the ferry tend to be discouraged and silly mistakes are often made.

Companies are often reluctant to employ older workers, particularly those over 50 years because they believe that they will be slower to learn new skills, as the quote goes 'you can't teach an old dog new tricks'. Porteous (1997) claims that older workers have problems adapting to new technology and keeping pace with fellow workers and machines. It is difficult to identify whether this is because of a decline in ability or a lack of motivation. Should employers discriminate on grounds of age?

1. Choose a job which seems basic and routine to you. Describe the basic skills involved.

2. Design a training programme to prepare an employee for this job.

**Review exercise**

## Summary

This chapter has focused on selection and training. It began by exploring the first steps in the process of selecting workers, job analysis and job specification. It then progressed to describe and evaluate methods of job selection including psychometric testing, biodata and interviewing. Intelligence tests, projective tests and the Eysenck and Cattell approaches to personality testing were discussed. The three components of training needs analysis were examined. These are organisational analysis, task analysis and person analysis. The application of learning theory in training situations was discussed.

## Further reading

Porteous, M. (1997) *Occupational Psychology*, Hemel Hempstead: Prentice Hall. Chapters 6–11. This text deals with these areas in detail and includes much research from European sources.

Warr, P. (ed.) (1987) *Psychology at Work* 3rd edn, London: Penguin. Chapter seven by Herriot gives a good overview of research into the interview situation.

Breakwell, G.M. (1989) *Interviewing*, Leicester: British Psychological Society. A practical guide to interviewing written as a tool for practitioners. An accessible text which includes practical exercises.

# 5

# Health and work

## Introduction

If you think back to Chapter 2 you will hopefully recall Warr's vitamin model where he looked at the effects of employment, or its absence, on the individual. Chapter 5 will explore this area in more depth. It will look initially at the relationship between work and health, and will focus on the topic of **stress** at work. It will then look at unemployment and retirement and their effects on health.

## Work and health

Warr (1987) indicated that having a job in western society can provide many basic needs and can be instrumental in influencing both physical and mental health. We will consider various factors which may affect both kinds of health.

## Physical risks

It has been recognised for many years that some occupations are hazardous by nature, such as the building trades which involve heavy physical labour and the use of heavy tools and machinery. Mining is obviously dangerous and workers enter the employment aware of the physical risks from working underground. Other long-term health risks from coal mining are now evident; inhaling coal dust has deleterious long-term effects and many miners become disabled and die young from lung diseases such as pneumoconiosis and emphysema. As medical knowledge advances these kinds of risk become easier to quantify and regulations are sometimes passed to minimise the risk, a process which has been ongoing for at least 150 years. As we saw in Chapter 1 the number of workers involved in manual occupations has decreased in western society and the emphasis has moved away from physical stress and towards psychological stress.

## Psychological and emotional risks

In 1991 the Confederation of British Industry, an organisation of owners, directors and managers, estimated that sickness absences from stress and mental disorders cost industry in the UK five billion pounds. The British Social Attitudes Survey (HMSO 1998 and 1999) asked employees aged 18 years and over about their attitudes to working conditions. They were asked to respond on a five-point scale ranging from always to never. The results (see Table 5.1) indicate that nine out of ten employees questioned felt that they sometimes came home from work feeling exhausted.

## Working hours

One issue that may affect both mental and physical health is the number of hours worked. In Chapter 1 you saw that 6-day weeks, consisting of 60 to 80 hours, were considered normal. As the nineteenth century progressed the number of hours were decreased as it was realised that the excessive working hours were a cause of poor health. The number of hours which individuals are expected to work in any week has decreased over the twentieth century. However the British still have the longest working week in the European community, they do an

*Table 5.1* Attitudes to working conditions

| | Always/ Often | Some- times | Hardly ever/ never | Can't choose/ not answered |
|---|---|---|---|---|
| **Come home from work exhausted** | 42 | 48 | 9 | 2 |
| **Find work stressful** | 33 | 46 | 20 | 1 |
| **Have to do hard physical work** | 22 | 26 | 51 | 1 |
| **Work in dangerous conditions** | 11 | 16 | 70 | 2 |

Source: HMSO (1998 and 1999).

average of 45 hours work per week in contrast to the Germans who work an average of 36 hours. Half of the male manual workers in the EEC who work over 48 hours a week are British. In 1998 over five million employees worked 48 hours or more per week in their main job. Opinion is divided about the effects of these hours. The Japanese accept that individuals can die from overwork and label this as **karoshi**, acknowledging it as a cause of death. Cooper and Cartwright (1995) suggest that long and irregular hours have an effect on happiness and health and have stated that presenteeism, the practice of being seen to work long hours, is the workplace disease of the 1990s. Statistical evidence suggests that the divorce rate in countries like the UK, where there is a long working week and a pattern of both partners in a relationship working full time, is higher than in similar countries where the working week is shorter. On the other hand the CBI states that the highest levels of absence from work occur among people who work a regular 37–40 hour week. The CBI believes that the majority of absences are caused by illness and family commitments.

### Shift work

There are general indications that shift work can be damaging to the individual's health and that shift workers are more likely to suffer from illnesses such as high blood pressure and gastrointestinal disorders than non-shift workers. Cszeisler *et al.* (1982) found that shift work amongst manual workers in an industrial setting in Utah, USA, was correlated with raised accident rates, absenteeism and chronic feelings of ill health. The existing shift pattern involved a change in the start and finish time every few days, in an irregular shift pattern. Cszeisler *et al.* suggested that shifts should run at the same time for 3 weeks and that the shift changes should move to a later time rather than an earlier one, i.e. a 6 am to 2 pm shift should move to 2 pm to 10 pm and so on. This system was adopted and as a result sickness and accident rates decreased and productivity increased by 22 per cent.

In contrast Hawkins and Armstrong-Esther's (1978) study of nurses indicated that there were individual differences in the ability to tolerate shift work and that some people actually prefer this way of working. However this study involved a small sample of workers.

### Employment status and health

It is acknowledged that some jobs are more stressful than others. A common perception is that managerial jobs are stressful because the individual has to take responsibility for decisions that affect others. Cooper and Cartwright (1995) published a survey for Times newspapers rating the level of stress of different occupations. The survey showed that miners, police officers and construction workers had the highest levels of stress, and vicars, astronomers and museum and library workers had the lowest levels. Another survey by the Health Education Authority (1988) listed the four most stressful jobs as nursing, social work, teaching and the police force. Most of these high-scoring jobs are in the public sector where workloads have increased considerably, while at the same time workers feel that their professional control over their workload has been diminished. These jobs involve contact with members of the public in circumstances which may lead to violent confrontation. In addition they carry high public expectations of standards of performance and, with the possible exception of the police force, either low government and/or low public esteem. The position of newly qualified hospital doctors who are required to work extremely long hours in unpredictable situations is a good illustration of this phenomenon. Cooper and Cartwright indicate that as the particular combination of stressors will vary, it is impossible to rank them in any meaningful way but the factors listed earlier are central in understanding stress. Increasing numbers of workers in these highly stressful jobs have successfully taken their employers to court, claiming that they became ill because of stress in the workplace, and the employer failed to acknowledge. However this is controversial and there are those who claim that unsafe physical environments, such as coal mining, are in fact more stressful.

### Health and control in the working environment

Government research (HMSO 1998 and 1999) and more recent work from Wilkinson (1986) have shown a relationship between occupation, ill health and death rates. It would appear that those workers who face constant uncertainty in their working environment and those who have little control over their workload find the environment most stressful. A study of the civil service by Marmot *et al.* (1982) showed that employees on the lowest employment grades were four times more likely to die of a heart attack than those on the most senior grades. They were also more likely to suffer from cancers, strokes and gastro-intestinal disorders. In fact there was a straightforward statistical relationship between employment grades and health, with the workers on the lowest grades, i.e. those with the least control over their circumstances at work, suffering the poorest health. It is important to note that all the workers in this study had white-collar jobs where there is little environmental risk, raising the possibility that blue-collar workers in dangerous environments may be even more seriously affected.

This research prompted Marmot *et al.* (1982) and Wilkinson (1986) to speculate about psychologically stressful working environments. They suggest that it is not purely the physical environment that is important for health but that other factors are equally important. Wilkinson suggests that the underlying problem is working in an environment where there is very little individual control and where there is also the perception of relative deprivation, a realisation that one is less well off in economic and social terms than the majority of the population. Both this and the previous example suggest that the individual's perception of their working situation and their placement within the social structure are powerful forces.

Progress exercise

List three factors in the working environment that may contribute to the mental and physical health of the individual.

## Stress at work

Stress at work used to be a topic that only interested academics and the medical profession. More recently it has become a concern of most employers as it is now known that stress impairs performance at work. As previously stated employees have successfully sued employers for causing illnesses by making them work in stressful environments. Stress management courses continue to proliferate to teach employees to 'manage' their workplace stress.

Perhaps a good starting point would be to define **stress**. It is a psychological and physiological response that occurs when an individual perceives that they are in a threatening situation. Stress is often experienced as a feeling of anxiety. **Anxiety** is a state of worry, fear or apprehension. It is a good evolutionary response and has developed to make us react to dangerous situations either by escaping or by finding ways of coping with the threat efficiently. When an individual perceives that they are under threat their sympathetic nervous system prepares them for flight or fight and they experience a range of physiological responses including rapid heart beat, sweating, 'butterflies' in the stomach, and increased levels of adrenaline and other body chemicals. These responses enable the body to react quickly and effectively to either deal with the stressor or escape from it. After meeting the stressor the body returns to a steady state. The response to stress is called an **adaptive response** because it increases the individual's potential to survive.

### Selye – the general adaptation syndrome

Selye (1956) believed that modern life presents situations where stress is ongoing and cannot be resolved. He suggested that the fight or flight response had evolved to cope effectively with short-term threats and that these would normally be followed by a period of rest to allow the body to recover. The consequences of a prolonged state of arousal would be exhaustion of the individual's physiological resources and immune system which would make the individual vulnerable to illness.

### Life events

Holmes and Rahe (1967) developed a social readjustment scale by listing **life events**, that is major changes or transitions in an individual's life. The list included both positive events, such as marriage, and negative ones, such as redundancy. Each event was given a notional score ranging from 11 for a minor legal violation to a maximum of 100 for the death of a spouse. Participants were asked to score themselves by adding up the total points change in a 12-month period. The number of illnesses, accidents and sports injuries in the following 12-month period were then recorded. Holmes and Rahe demonstrated a positive correlation between the life-events score and the number of illnesses and accidents. The higher the life-events score the greater the risk to the individual. Becoming unemployed, changing jobs, changing responsibilities at work and a wife beginning work are all on the scale.

#### Commentary on the life-events scale

The last factor mentioned above leads to the first comment. The scale was designed with male workers in mind and was tested out on naval personnel in the USA. One must therefore question its generalisability to women and to different cultural settings. In addition Holmes and Rahe underestimated the role of cognitive factors, as did Selye. Whilst their figures may be accurate when looking at the wider picture they fail to account for individual differences. Some people can cope with a great deal of stress and endure horrific life events without becoming ill, whilst others are knocked off course very easily. What may be important is not just the life event itself but its meaning and significance for the individual. A planned and welcome life event which is 'on time', that is one which occurs at the appropriate time in a particular culture, will be less stressful than an unplanned, unexpected 'off time' event. A planned retirement from work may be viewed positively whereas an unplanned, unexpected redundancy notice will have the opposite effect.

It would also seem reasonable to suggest that the job itself has an effect, regardless of life events. It has already been suggested that nurses, teachers and the lower grade civil servants are suffering from stress because they perceive that their workload is out of their control and that society fails to reward them in both pecuniary and status terms. This type of continuous, ongoing stress or 'hassle' as Lazarus and Folkman (1984) label it may be more damaging than life events. There are also indications that each of us has a different capacity to cope with stress and that this will depend on both our personality and previous life experiences.

### Stress hardiness

Lazarus and Folkman (1984) emphasised cognitive factors and suggested that the change in life events or the threat which someone is facing, may be less important than the individual's perception of their ability to cope. If you are working in a casualty department the risk of being attacked can be quantified statistically, but an individual's perception of that threat can not. Kobasa (1982) indicates that the interaction between the individual and the social situation is always unique because of differences in ability to deal with stressful situations. She claims that some individuals are more stress hardy than others and has listed the successful strategies which they use. Stress-hardy individuals are more actively involved in their work and social lives, they believe that they are in control of events and respond well to challenges. She links stress hardiness with early experiences and states that these successful strategies are the product of learning.

### Commentary on workplace stress

Porteous (1997) questions the link between stress and health risks. He states that it is difficult to separate factors such as inherited family characteristics and health risks and life-style choices such as diet or smoking from the effects of stress in the workplace. Friedman *et al.* (1995) followed up research by Terman and Oden (1947). The initial longitudinal study, started in 1921, involved a cohort of gifted children (the Termites) in the USA and claimed to find a correlation between the personality characteristics of the Termites and their general health and life expectancy. By 1990 half the group had died. Friedman studied their death certificates and correlated the findings with the personality factors identified in the earlier study. Those identified as truthful, dependable and prudent in early childhood lived longer than those identified as impulsive and lacking in social control. Also those whose parents divorced and who had unhappy marriages themselves had a life expectancy 4 years shorter than those from stable homes who had good marriages. It is also worthy of note that the truthful and dependable individuals were less likely to smoke or drink and fewer of them had died in accidents or violent incidents. This is a correlational study that looks at a relationship between personality and illness and, although it is difficult to claim cause and effect, it does suggest that the working environment is only one of many possible variables involved in the genesis of both mental and physical illness. It leads us to ask if stress itself causes illness or if people react to stress by smoking, drinking and eating poorly and consequently damaging their health.

Stress at work is said to have increased in the 1980s and 1990s. Discuss two factors in the workplace which cause stress and suggest ways of modifying the work environment to reduce stress.

*Progress exercise*

## Unemployment

The number of people unemployed varies as the economy fluctuates between prosperity and depression. The impact of unemployment is not felt evenly in western societies. Unskilled manual workers are more likely to lose their jobs than workers with high levels of skill or in professional jobs, they then find it more difficult to become re-employed and may remain unemployed for a considerable period of time. Those in the upper middle class are significantly less likely to lose a job and will find re-employment more easily. In 1998 workers with no qualifications were four times more likely to be unemployed than those with higher education qualifications. Young workers and those over 50 years old are more vulnerable. Employers do not want someone without work experience and fear that older workers may be inflexible and unfit. Young unskilled workers lose out because employers dislike their lack of experience and do not want to take training costs on board. They prefer an individual who is already trained and has some real experience of work.

## Effects of unemployment

The most obvious consequence of unemployment for most people is the loss of income. Very few individuals have private means, and state benefits, if they are available, are intended to provide only the basic necessities. The effect of having no job in a society where working is the expected norm has been researched since the 1930s. Jahoda (1958) drew attention to the psychological effects of unemployment. After surveying unemployed men in Europe she concluded that there were links between prolonged periods of unemployment and the incidence of depression and apathy. Her conclusions were influential in developing social policy towards the unemployed but they did not remove the unfortunate stereotype that unemployed people are lazy and not working by choice. Within western society there is an assumption that anyone can find work if they really want to and, to quote Norman Tebbitt, should 'get on their bikes and look for work'.

Subsequent studies have confirmed the ill effects of unemployment in males. As stated in Chapter 2, Moser *et al.* (1984) analysed the mortality rates in males aged 15–64 years, between 1971 and 1981, and found that the unemployed males were significantly more likely to die young than employed males. A study by Warr and Jackson (1985) showed that between 20 and 30 per cent of the unemployed men they surveyed reported increased levels of anxiety, lack of confidence, irritability, insomnia and listlessness. They also reported increases in physical conditions, which are thought to be linked to emotional ill health, such as skin disorders, ulcers and headaches. However 10 per cent of the sample reported a perception of improved health. These were workers who had illnesses which were aggravated by their working conditions and who therefore felt better when able to leave their jobs.

Seabrook's (1982) study of redundancies in steel workers in south Wales showed a good initial response to unemployment, particularly where people had received a large lump sum of compensation for giving up their job. However, the long-term effects were bad. To quote someone who lived in one of the south Wales towns 'it was like the Klondike for a while – a real boomtown, and then it all fell to pieces'. Fryer and Payne (1984) had difficulty in finding any individuals who had reacted positively to unemployment.

### The Beale study

The Beale and Nethercott (1985) study of unemployment in a Wiltshire town presents a clear picture of the links between unemployment and health. In 1987 the Harris meat processing plant in Calne closed. It was the main employer in Calne, a small Wiltshire town, and the workers were given 2 years' notice of the factory closure. A local GP studied the results of the closure by comparing the health records of workers who were being made redundant with a control group in the town who were still in work. He found marked differences in the mental and physical health of the two groups. The workers who were made redundant had a significant increase in the number of consultations and a sixfold increase in referrals to specialists for serious illnesses. It was noted that these increases started as soon as the redundancy notices were received, rather than at the start of the period of unemployment, indicating that psychological factors were of paramount importance. This study looked at all workers and found more pronounced effects in females than in males. The partners and children of workers were also affected.

Beale and Nethercott's study, which was very well designed, showed a clear link between both unemployment and the threat of unemployment and health. Unfortunately funding was not available to follow up the patients over a longer period but the findings appear to confirm the existing research on the deleterious effects on losing one's job.

### Other research into unemployment

More recent research in the UK has focused on young unemployed males. The risk of suicide in young males has increased consistently since the mid-1980s. The unemployed are at the highest risk in this group and para-suicide (attempted suicide) has shown a similar increase. The increase has been so marked that reducing the suicide rate in young males is now an official government health aim. It is difficult to draw firm conclusions about this problem, as it may be that the factors which precipitated the suicide were also responsible for the unemployment. Whilst it is always difficult to disentangle explanations of suicide in any individual the data indicate a relationship overall between unemployment and suicide.

### Overview

An overview of the research does indicate links between unemployment and mental health. In times of prosperity, when unemployment rates are low, it is possible that unemployed people may represent a group who are generally at high risk of poor health because the same factors are causing both the unemployment and the poor physical and mental health.

Studies from periods of high unemployment, such as those completed by Jahoda in the 1930s (Jahoda *et al*. 1933) and the research listed above from the 1980s and 1990s, suggest that differences in health between employed and unemployed people are related to the experience of job loss and the inability to gain further employment.

Progress exercise

List three negative factors which an individual might experience as a result of becoming unemployed.

## Retirement

Many industrialised societies have unfavourable stereotypes of the elderly. The elderly are more likely to suffer from poor health, often have low levels of income and are perceived as being less physically attractive than young people. As retirement is seen to mark the start of old age it is not surprising that many view it negatively.

To return to Chapter 1 it was, and still is in many places, expected that an individual would work for as long as they could and that even when they were physically unfit to work they would be consulted by those still able to work. With industrialisation employers became increasingly unwilling to offer jobs to the physically less fit, and families found it increasingly difficult to provide for aged relatives who could not earn. This led to the introduction of pensions as a way of ensuring that those who were unable to work because of old age had some form of income. An agreed retirement age then followed and a system became established where people above a certain age are no longer expected to work. Retirement then becomes a life event and is a potential cause of stress.

In the UK retirement is expected to occur between the ages of 60 and 65 years but an increasing number of people leave employment either earlier or later than this. Some take early retirement from choice but many are made redundant and would have chosen to continue working if they could. This means that it is difficult to distinguish between the consequences of retirement and redundancy (unemployment) in the 50 to 65-year age group. Similarly some individuals work into their seventies and beyond. This is particularly true of those in professional jobs such as the legal profession. Members of Parliament are another such group. The timing of retirement therefore can vary by as much as 30 years and this is another factor making it difficult to come to firm conclusions about retirement and health.

### Atchley's phases of retirement

Atchley (1991) has produced a model that suggests there are seven phases to describe an individual's approach to retirement.

1. *Remote*   Retirement is a long time away and the individual does not give it much thought.
2. *Near retirement*   As the individual approaches retirement s/he begins to make plans and consider his/her future.
3. *The honeymoon phase*   The individual has retired and is enjoying his/her new-found freedom. S/he may take up new activities or spend more time on activities which s/he enjoys, such as travel or spending time with grandchildren.

4. *Disenchantment* For some individuals the initial pleasure wears off and s/he feels disappointed and let down. Retirement has not produced what was expected.
5. *Reorientation* The individual reviews her/his life and adapts to a changed life style.
6. *Stability* The individual has fully adjusted to his/her role. This could be understood in terms of Warr's concept of environmental clarity, that is the degree to which a person is confident and secure in their physical and psychological surroundings. To remind yourself of this concept it may be useful to refer back to Chapter 2.
7. *Terminal* This final phase occurs when the retirement role ends. Some individuals may return to work. Others may become so ill or dependent that they cannot care for themselves. At this stage they may begin to prepare for death.

### Commentary on Atchley

These are phases not stages and not all individuals will experience them all. They present a description of the retirement process in western, industrialised society. Other factors, which are also vitally important, are the individual's financial status and their health. A rich, healthy person is likely to experience retirement in a very different way to a poor person with long-term health problems. The presence or absence of close relatives will also have an effect. In the 1950s Townsend (1957) carried out an extensive study of the family life of elderly people in London and established the importance of contact with relatives in terms of both their physical and emotional welfare. The elderly who had contact with relatives were happier and less likely to need assistance from the state. His recommendations, that wherever possible the elderly should be housed close to their near kin, were accepted as good practice by Social Service and Housing Departments and the policies are still in place. People who have moved away from their extended families for employment and those whose children have moved away, often for similar reasons, are likely to be affected in a more negative way by retirement once they become frail or ill. Bereavement is more likely to occur at this stage and the combination of loss of job and loss of partner is particularly damaging.

Research from Germany (Baltes 1990) suggests that the overriding factor affecting the quality of life after retirement is the person's perception of the situation and their perception of being in control. You may find it useful therefore to consider some of the issues raised about stress earlier in this chapter and apply them to this area.

> Discuss the effects of either unemployment or retirement on the individual. You may find it useful to look at both positive and negative aspects of these life events.

*Review exercise*

## Summary

This chapter has focused on health and work. It referred back to Warr's vitamin model in terms of the positive effects of work on health. The effects of working conditions on both mental and physical health were considered. Issues including physical hazards, working hours and shift work were then examined. The role of stress in the workplace and its links with working hours was considered. Links between social class, particular occupational groups and stress were also examined. It was noted that studies of stress in Great Britain indicated that low-status work carried higher risks than management and that workers in the public sector reported high levels of stress. In both cases the difficulties of generalisation were apparent. The effects of unemployment and retirement on health were then introduced, including studies from Beale and Atchley. Again the importance of individual differences within overall trends must be taken into account.

## Further reading

Fontana, D. (1987) *Managing Stress*, London: Tavistock. A short, easily read text that is a good introduction to the general area of stress. It contains a stress assessment exercise which you can apply to yourself.

Carlson, N.R. and Buskist, W. (1997) *Psychology. The Science of Behaviour* 5th edn, Needham Heights, MA: Allyn and Bacon.

Chapter 16, Life style, Stress and Health, provides a relevant and highly readable introduction to this area of psychology.

Wilkinson, R.G. (ed.) (1986) *Class and Health. Research and Longitudinal Data*, London: Tavistock. Although mainly concerned with links between social class and health this text contains relevant studies of the effects of employment status and health.

Warr, P. (1987) *Work, Unemployment and Mental Health*, Oxford: Oxford University Press. This text presents a detailed examination of the area and covers data from a wide range of cultures and sources. It is a university text and is therefore less accessible than the source mentioned above.

# Groups and decision making

## Introduction

Human beings have evolved to live in groups. Although psychology focuses on individual behaviour, humans spend much time in the company of others. One of the vitamins that Warr named was 'valued social contact'. Maslow listed social needs and McClelland gave a need for affiliation as an important motivator for human behaviour.

## Social identity theory

Tajfel (1978) suggests that there are two components to our self-image or identity. One is our **personal identity**, i.e. our personal characteristics and **traits**. The other component is our **social identity**, this derives from the social groups to which we belong and our membership of these social groups affects how we see ourselves. Often in self-description people will state not only their actual job but also the organisation that employs them. For example in the army a soldier will identify her/himself by the regiment s/he belongs to. Two individuals with the same job may see their identity in very different ways 'I work on the till in a supermarket' and 'I am a cashier at a famous west end store' send out different messages about social identity although both jobs are basically the same. Group identity is also central to understanding the way in which any organisation functions.

Tajfel states that social interactions can be defined along a continuum between interpersonal and intergroup perspectives. In other words, there are occasions when our behaviour is driven and motivated by our self-perception. An example of this is interactions between parents and their teenage children, where the dialogues are based on personal knowledge and, hopefully, an understanding of each other's position. Conflict resolution is likely to be negotiated and will be resolved according to the demands of the individual situation.

At other times we act in accordance with our social identity. For example a parent, who is a member of the police force, is likely to react differently to a group of rioting adolescent football fans than they would react to their own children. Similarly the adolescent's perception of, and behaviour towards, the adult is likely to be different. It is likely that, when acting on the basis of social identity, both groups will be working from stereotypes. The police officer and the football fan will not see each other as individuals but will rely on fixed and inflexible beliefs about each other's characteristics and intentions. A great number of negotiations and responses are driven by group identity rather than individual needs.

In general terms, we try to be reasonable and negotiate in situations where we are acting in personal terms. When we are acting as group members, we tend to respond in stereotypical ways and often behave in accordance with group demands.

You may be aware of occasions when you have become involved in activities with a group that you would not indulge in on your own. This could be an occasion where you are celebrating and hug everyone in sight because your sports team has won an event, or it could be antisocial behaviour such as bullying. It may be useful to try to analyse your social and personal self in this context. Which is the real you? Perhaps they both are.

*Progress exercise*

### Commentary on social identity theory

The desire to conform to group pressure is very high. This was shown many years ago in an experiment by Asch (1956) in which university students were given the simple task of choosing two lines of matching length from a list of several lines. They were placed in a panel with seven confederates of the experimenter who all gave the same, obviously incorrect answer claiming that two lines of unequal length were identical. The unsuspecting students were last in line. When their turn came to answer the majority chose to give the same wrong answer. It appeared that this was easier to do than departing from the group consensus. The pressure of a group, even if you do not know them well, can be very strong. Interestingly engineers will insist that the lines are not equal and will give the correct response. Perrin and Spencer (1981) suggest that accuracy in measurement is a basic and essential skill for an engineer and that giving a wrong answer would be a denial of his/her personal identity. This indicates that our position on the continuum between self and social identity will depend on both the strength of our individual views and the social pressure in any given situation. The pressure of peer groups in working situations is vital to productivity and the Japanese working culture relies heavily on creating a strong social identification with the workplace.

### Groups

Group membership, such as that of a group of colleagues, can be central to our identity. The efficient co-operation of individuals in groups is central to successful organisational functioning. Social identity theory suggests that groups are fundamental to self identity. It may be useful to define the term **group**. One common definition is that a group consists of two or more persons who share a common purpose or function. A football *crowd* would meet these criteria but it is too large. A small number of football supporters together are a group. At what point do they become a crowd? It may be useful to introduce the idea that a group consists of a small number of people who engage in meaningful social contact. Furnham (1997) states that groups have four defining characteristics

1. they consist of two or more interacting individuals who will be able to influence each other's ideas and behaviour
2. they share common goals
3. they exist over a period of time and have a relatively stable structure
4. the group members recognise themselves as a group and group membership will be acknowledged.

Groups at work may be formal and employers may define workers as members of a particular team. They may also be informal and consist of individuals who have common social interests at work or who may be friendly outside the work setting. It is possible for the needs of the formal and informal groups to be in conflict.

### Group formation

How does an individual become part of a group? There are a number of models which attempt to explain this and it is obviously important for understanding the psychology of organisations. Tuckman (1965) suggests that there are five stages of group formation.

1. *Forming*  When the members of the group first meet they will focus on defining a common goal or a series of goals which they can not achieve independently. The group may have chosen to get together to achieve certain goals or they may be a group of strangers meeting for an externally imposed purpose. The needs of the individual will therefore come second to the overall purpose of the group. Group members may well feel confused and uncertain at this point and any hostility or aggression may be concealed until they have assessed the costs and benefits to themselves. A set of rules or norms will

begin to emerge and these will be used to define the group's purpose and help it to work as a unit.

2. *Storming* The group begins to work towards its goal, and as the members get to know each other they become more confident about their individual roles; however, conflicts may arise about the purpose of the group. Some individuals may accept compromises to allow the group to go forward while others may feel that their opinions are not being considered. If leaders have not been formally appointed at the start they may emerge at this point. The group may fail if key members withdraw. If conflict is suppressed rather than resolved there are likely to be problems in the long term.

3. *Norming* The group then becomes 'we' and acknowledges that the whole is greater than the sum of its parts. Group members will focus on resolving the differences in the previous stage and those who are still not in agreement will either compromise or leave, if they can. A group identity will emerge and both formal and informal rules will be established. If this is achieved to the satisfaction of group members and without too many feeling coerced into acceptance, the group can begin to formulate plans and work to the accepted goal/s. Those who then do not conform to group norms will quickly be brought into line. Different groups often adapt very different strategies and norms in pursuit of the same goal.

4. *Performing* The group now gets on with the task in hand, and energy previously used up in conflict resolution and norm setting can be diverted into action. Group members will be expected to comply with the norms and newcomers will be expected to conform rather than question. At this stage some groups may become extremely effective. Others, where conflicts have not been resolved or who have developed norms which are unsupportive of effectiveness, may perform poorly. Membership of a group is not necessarily productive.

5. *Adjourning* Once the task is completed, for example at the end of a course, the group will break up. This can also occur when group members decide for other reasons that they no longer have a common purpose. If the group splits without animosity this may be referred to as the mourning phase and may leave members feeling miserable and nostalgic. They may decide to have a ceremony to mark the group splitting up, such as a party, and will often make plans for a reunion at this point.

Progress exercise

You may have experienced the process of group formation in the past. Starting or leaving school or college shows many of the features detailed above. Describe your experience using the above stages.

## Organisational socialisation

When individuals share common goals and/or environments, group formation is an inevitable product of social interaction. When people start work, join an organisation or a social group, they become part of a group which is already established. They are therefore socialised into the expectations of the organisation. This may occur formally, through a period of training and induction, or on a very informal basis. Feldman (1976) examined this process and described three stages:

1. *Anticipatory* The newcomer wants to find out about the organisation and see where they will fit in.
2. *Accommodation* The individual learns about her/his job and position in the organisation. S/he will learn about her/his own place in the organisation and about the roles of others. Some of these roles will be formally defined and may be a part of the job title, for example manager, trainee, health and safety officer. Others may be much more informal and it may take the newcomer some time to recognise them, for example office gossip or the person you can trust to give you good advice.
3. *Role management* The individual knows the parameters of their own and other people's jobs and becomes a member of the team in the workplace.

Organisational psychologists and human resource departments are often involved in planning this process to ensure that the new employee fits in well. You may remember going through a process of induction when starting a new job or joining an educational establishment.

Progress exercise

Design an induction programme for someone joining a workplace or educational establishment. What will you put into the programme? How long will it last?

## Decision making

Once formed are groups wiser than individuals? Common sense tells us that problem solving and decision making are often done best in groups, on the premise that groups will come to more sensible and realistic decisions than an individual. Although the Prime Minister is the leader of the UK s/he is only 'first among equals' and the members of the cabinet are supposed to discuss all major decisions. Most large companies have a board of directors, a group of people to whom the managers are answerable. Popular wisdom has two opposing views on this. I was taught when young 'two heads are better than one, even if one's nobbut a sheep's head' but I was also familiar with the claim 'a camel is a horse designed by a committee'. Which of these views is correct? Let us look at some evidence.

Miller (1989) suggests that the decision-making process will reflect both the type of decision to be made and its importance. The owner of a company is hardly likely to use the same rules and strategies when deciding where to go for a meal with her/his friends as s/he is when about to make a multi-million pound investment which may affect the future of hundreds of workers. In the first case a consensus decision is likely to be reached and the individual will happily go along with the majority decision without too much argument. The consequence of having a meal you do not enjoy is likely to be no more than short-term annoyance. As the second decision has long-term, serious implications for a large number of people the individual will probably be involved in prolonged discussions with all interested parties but will eventually take an independent decision. Similarly the relative significance of the decision affects groups. Where there is no clear-cut correct answer a majority decision will usually suffice. If a jury can not reach a unanimous verdict then they may be asked to reconsider and a majority verdict will be accepted. However if a factual issue is at stake then the individual/s who produce the right answer are likely to have their view accepted, even if they start off as a minority.

### Group polarisation – the risky shift

The logic behind group decision making is that each individual will bring their specialist knowledge to the situation and therefore the total expertise will be greater than that of one individual. However groups usually take longer than individuals to reach a decision and this may, at best, be inefficient and, at worst, dangerous. It is also presumed that extremism is more likely to be kept in check by group decision making. This latter possibility has been queried in a well-known psychological phenomenon known as the **risky shift**, first described by Stoner (1961). Individuals in laboratory conditions are asked to discuss a series of dilemmas with a choice of two options. They are asked individually to calculate which option should be taken and choose a range of odds on the success or failure of each option. The individuals are then placed in groups of six and asked to reconsider their decisions. See Figure 6.1 for a typical example.

After discussion most individuals moved towards choosing a greater risk. Brown (1986) suggests that two factors explain this phenomenon, namely 'social comparison' and 'persuasive argument'. He suggests that both must be present for the shift to occur. Social comparison is the process of comparing your decision with that of others in the group and it may cause you to shift in order to conform to the others. Persuasive argument is the process of expressing and sharing views and then coming to a decision. If you refer to the study by Asch (1956) it should help you to understand this process. The initial research showed movement in a risky direction, hence the name 'risky shift'. Later research demonstrated that the shift resulting from this process could be either in the direction of risk or caution depending on the circumstances leading to the group polarisation. In group settings responsibility for a decision is not always easy to identify and it is easier for a group member with more extreme views to push a particular viewpoint without appearing responsible for it.

Mr A has been employed by the same large engineering company since leaving university. The company have good, if unexciting, long-term prospects and are paying him an adequate wage with good fringe benefits including an excellent pension scheme. Mr A is married, he is the sole wage earner and has one child.

Through contacts at a conference Mr A is offered alternative employment with a small, newly established company. At the moment the new company's future is uncertain. If they succeed they could become a large, highly profitable unit but there is also a high risk that the business will fail if things do not go to plan.

Mr A is offered a much higher salary than he is on at present, plus the potential of share options and profit sharing should the company succeed. There is no pension scheme.

Choose from the following options to decide at which point Mr A should be advised to take the new job.

1. The chances are 1 in 10 that the company will prove financially sound.

2. The chances are 3 in 10 that the company will prove financially sound.

3. The chances are 5 in 10 that the company will prove financially sound.

4. The chances are 7 in 10 that the company will prove financially sound.

5. The chances are 9 in 10 that the company will prove financially sound.

*Figure 6.1* **The risky shift example**

*Commentary on the risky shift*

This research was based on discussions in a laboratory situation and the individuals had neither emotional involvement with the decision nor did they have to face any consequences from the decision. One must therefore query the validity of the application of this phenomenon in real life. One must also take into consideration environmental factors. If you return to Mr A it is not implausible to suggest that a group choosing odds when the economy is depressed will be likely to take smaller risks than one working when the economy is buoyant.

### *Groupthink*

The phenomenon known as **groupthink** (Janis 1982; see Chapter 8, Study aids) is where politicians and others have taken joint decisions which have proved extremely foolish with hindsight, one of the most famous being Pearl Harbor when the USA ignored indications that the Japanese were about to invade Hawaii. Groupthink occurs when groups are under threat and isolated from outside sources of opinion. The group members become increasingly cohesive and any dissent is quickly smothered. They share a conviction that their view of the world is both correct and morally right, leading to the discrediting of information which deviates from the consensus. The desire for unanimity overrides normal, rational decision-making processes culminating in poor, often disastrous, decisions. A new product may be designed and the company will ignore market research which states that no one will buy it. Alternatively they may ignore new products on the market and continue to produce items to a shrinking market, convinced that they are right. This is what happened to the British motor-cycle industry in the face of competition from Japan. More recently in the UK the combined approach of the government and the Civil Service to the BSE (bovine spongiform encephalitis or 'mad cow disease') crisis illustrates the same point. There was a consensus that the issue was not really serious, leading to a refusal to listen to experts, and a conviction that keeping information secret would avoid panic.

Juries show decision making in real life situations. Lamm and Myers (1978) studied jurors and found that those who were convinced of a defendant's innocence of guilt before the jury went into discussion were even more adamant about their decision afterwards. Although the decision-making process of juries is confidential one can look at factors which affect their decisions. For example Kerr and Bray (1982) state that harsh penalties will lead to a fall in conviction rates. The presence of a mandatory death penalty will make a jury less likely to convict. Michelini and Snodgrass (1980) found that appearance had an effect and that physically attractive defendants were more likely to be acquitted. It may be that choices in employment are made in the same way and that decisions which appear to be financial are often driven by other, unacknowledged factors. One employee may be kept on because their employer is concerned about their home circumstances while another may be selected for redundancy on the grounds of their physical appearance.

Discuss two psychological studies of decision-making processes in groups.

## Group cohesiveness

Cohesiveness is literally the process of sticking together, and groups that are closely knit are referred to as cohesive. To return to the beginning of this chapter the suggestion was made that the groups we belong to form a vital part of our picture of ourselves. Hogg (1992) suggests that groups become cohesive when the group acknowledges mutual interdependence and the members view each other as a source of reward and the means to achieve mutually desired goals. Until recently Japanese work culture involved offering an individual a job for life within the organisation in return for loyalty. For some workers being an employee of Honda or a similar company was an integral part of their self-image. The organisation was a cohesive whole and this was presumed to increase both personal satisfaction and productivity.

Public schools in the UK also work on a similar basis, using team games and house systems to cement relationships. This identity often lasts through life after the individual has left the organisation: men of pensionable age still identify themselves as old Etonians! Most of the uniformed services work in a similar way. Probably one of the best descriptions of the process can be found in the book called *Asylums* by Goffman (see Further reading, p. 95). Goffman studied a range of large institutions, including psychiatric hospitals and prisons, and observed a strong process of socialisation taking place. For example there were procedures on admission to these units, such as showering and issuing uniforms, which Goffman felt were aimed at destroying the individual's former identity and establishing them as a prisoner or patient. These processes led to the establishment of highly polarised, cohesive groups which held negative stereotypes of each other and had profound effects on behaviour. A great deal of energy was expended by both groups trying to get one over on the other and there were very high levels of mutual suspicion and hostility.

Tajfel and Turner (1979) indicate that we view our own group as superior to others and will favour them at the expense of others. If resources are scarce we will distribute them to the advantage of the group we belong to.

## Intergroup conflict

An organisation may be either a cohesive whole or a number of groups which hold positive or negative stereotypes of each other. Conflict between workers and management illustrates this and, in the extreme, it can produce strikes or other forms of industrial action which could destroy the whole organisation.

Organisations may function as a number of separate groups which hold positive or negative stereotypes of each other. Conflict can then occur between these groups. The armed forces, for example, have officers, non-commissioned officers, other ranks and civilians. Although the primary identification of each individual may be with the larger group (the armed forces) it is in the smaller group that they will function on a day-to-day basis, and the demands of the larger and smaller groups may not be the same. This can create conflict and structures need to be put in place to prevent this happening. Furnham indicates that particular leadership styles can either exacerbate or lessen conflict. A highly autocratic and dogmatic leader who attempts to prevent dissent may provoke extreme conflict in the long term as resentment builds up. Alternatively an open style of leadership may become counter productive, particularly where there are groups with radically differing value systems within one organisation. Most companies build in structures to minimise conflict, for example works councils, made up of representatives of the separate groups who meet to disseminate information and to improve understanding.

One technique which was developed after World War Two, and which is still widely used, is that of the T or Training group. This technique, which has changed and developed over the years, consists of allowing groups of individuals to interact in an unstructured way in order to allow them to gain insight into the effectiveness of their own social interactions and to give them an understanding of group dynamics.

Groups of football fans at away fixtures often show very high levels of social cohesion. Why should this be so?

**Role conflict** which can occur in the workplace can cause high stress levels for the individual. For example in industrial settings the demands of the organisation for higher productivity or lower wage bills may be in direct conflict with the needs of the workers, who may be highly resistant to the idea of working longer hours for smaller rewards. An individual in this setting may well feel conflict, if they do not accept the company's offer their job may disappear. If they do take it they may no longer have enough money to keep their existing standard of living. The increased hours may conflict with other demands from their family or they may fear for their health. In general terms intergroup conflict and role conflict produce negative outcomes for both the individual and the organisation.

## Teamwork

### Effective and ineffective teams

The term team is often used in the workplace to denote either a group of individuals who share a common purpose, for example the marketing team, or a group who are called together to complete a specific task. This latter definition will be used here. The theories and research already discussed have obvious implications here but it is also useful to look at research into what makes an effective team.

Psychological research does not always indicate those areas where it is more useful to work in teams (Furnham 1997). There is no doubt, however, that teams allow for the pooling of expertise and resources and can improve the morale and commitment of those involved in them. However teams also have powerful potential for time wasting and the individuals involved may feel that they would be better employed getting on with their own job rather than engaging in group decision making. None the less it is usual for managers to work in teams and group decisions are often seen as more rational and acceptable than those made by individuals. The truth is that group decisions are not always rational and one can encounter the risky shift phenomenon.

### Belbin – the characteristics of successful teams

Belbin (1981) suggested that successful teams have a number of salient characteristics.

1. The team leader's role is vital. S/he should be trustworthy and use the team's personal resources effectively and inspire confidence in other team members.
2. The team should include individuals with a wide range of skills and abilities. If everyone is clever then too much time can be spent on discussion. Without bright individuals there is often no spark.
3. Teams often function best when they contain an individual who is highly creative and can approach problems in an innovative way. The maverick can be useful in groups.

## Social facilitation and social inhibition

Being part of a team has been shown to both improve and damage the performance of individuals. Over a hundred years ago Tripplett (1898) suggested that the presence of competitors will improve performance. He asked children to reel in a fishing line and discovered that they performed the task faster when there were others doing the same task alongside them than they did when performing on their own. The presence of others **facilitated** or improved their performance.

It is well accepted in sports such as athletics that a competitor will run faster than someone can on their own. The first 4-minute mile, run by Roger Bannister, was achieved with the assistance of other athletes who acted as pacemakers by taking it in turns to run with him.

There are also occasions when the presence of others can damage performance. If an individual is highly nervous and has to perform a complicated task which they are unsure of then the presence of others may **inhibit** their performance and make it worse. If someone is required to play a musical instrument at a concert and they feel that they have had insufficient practice they will make even more errors than usual. Appearing for an examination in an unprepared state frequently has the same effect!

Zajonc (1965) has produced an explanation for these seemingly contradictory findings. He confirms that the presence of others has an effect on performance and that it increases our level of emotional arousal. The difference lies in our level of capability and in the difficulty of the task. If we have to complete a task which we have learned thoroughly and we feel extremely competent then the presence of others is likely to improve or *facilitate* our performance. If, however, we are not sure what we are doing and fear that we will make mistakes then the presence of others is likely to impair or *inhibit* our performance. This implies that groups and group tasks need careful monitoring if they are to be performed efficiently in the workplace. We need to make sure that the group is going to be more productive than several individuals working separately.

### Social loafing

During your time in the education system or at work you will have experienced the phenomenon of **social loafing**. Williams *et al.* (1993: 131) defines it as 'a reduction in individual effort when working on a collective task (in which one's outputs are pooled with those of other group members) compared to working either alone or coactively'.

Once one becomes a group member group loafing suggests that we can hide effectively and either leave the hard work to others or loaf together as a group, as no one individual will be held personally responsible for the group's work.

#### Empirical evidence

Social loafing is a phenomenon which has been extensively researched and which has been shown to occur in varying tasks, across different age groups and in a range of cultural settings. Ringlemann (1913) created a mock tug-of-war situation with two, three or eight members in the teams. He discovered that the effort made by each man decreased as the number of people in the team increased. More recently Latane *et al.* (1979) have created the same effect with tasks such as shouting, cheering and clapping. The implications here are that a group charged with a task will be less productive than a number of individuals. However these tasks were all artificial. It is particularly difficult to generalise from groups of American college students involving themselves in clapping and cheering exercises to productivity in a workplace.

*Explanations for loafing*

Green (1991) suggests three explanations for loafing.

1. *Output equity* Group members expect their colleagues to loaf and do so themselves to avoid being the one who makes all the effort.
2. *Evaluation apprehension* Group members may be anonymous and will not therefore be asked to explain their performance on an individual basis. No one is monitoring individual performance and no one can therefore be held responsible. This is particularly likely when the task is boring or appears to have little real purpose.
3. *Matching to standard* Group members have no indication of the standard that the task is supposed to produce. If completion criteria are unclear then loafing is likely.

From this it is possible to adapt strategies to avoid group loafing. Personal involvement, meaningful tasks, intergroup competition, and the possibility of individual identification all help to avoid group loafing. In the final chapter of this book, the role of leaders and the question of group decision making are discussed.

Progress exercise

Social loafing is often observed in classrooms when students are asked to work in groups. What steps could teachers take to prevent it happening?

## Communication in groups

One of the most influential pieces of work on communication in groups was produced by Bavelas (1950) who produced an article exploring the effects of communication patterns in groups, speed of information transfer and member satisfaction (see Figure 6.2).

GROUP CHARACTERISTICS

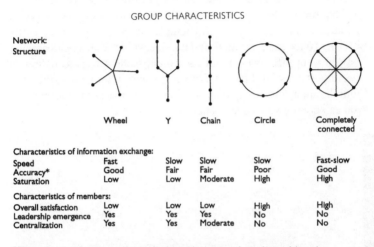

| Network: Structure | Wheel | Y | Chain | Circle | Completely connected |
|---|---|---|---|---|---|
| **Characteristics of information exchange:** | | | | | |
| Speed | Fast | Slow | Slow | Slow | Fast-slow |
| Accuracy* | Good | Fair | Fair | Poor | Good |
| Saturation | Low | Low | Moderate | High | High |
| **Characteristics of members:** | | | | | |
| Overall satisfaction | Low | Low | Low | High | High |
| Leadership emergence | Yes | Yes | Yes | No | No |
| Centralization | Yes | Yes | Moderate | No | No |

*These accuracy estimates may change according to the nature and complexity of the task.

*Figure 6.2* Communication patterns in groups (reprinted with permission from Bavelas, A. (1950) Communication patterns in task-oriented groups, *Journal of the Acoustical Society of America* 22, 725–30. Acoustical Society of America 1950).

It can be seen from Figure 6.2 that the structure of a group has profound effects on its functioning. For example structures which enable accurate communication to take place rapidly, such as the wheel, have low levels of satisfaction, whereas more democratic structures such as the circle are well liked by group members but are less efficient in terms of speed and accuracy of information transmission. Furnham (1997) suggests that those networks with the leader in the centre, such as the wheel, work best when the task in hand is simple. Those where the leader's position is difficult to identify and where there are links between all personnel, such as the circle, perform best with more complex tasks. Although this model fits small groups best it can be applied to larger organisations. Unfortunately it is becoming rapidly outdated with the use of modern technology such as the internet and intranet communication. It is possible for leaders to contact all members of an organisation whenever they wish to disseminate work-related information and for those workers to respond. It is also possible for all workers to communicate with each other and for a disgruntled employee to gain access to the whole workforce in an instant.

This means that organisations will have to adapt new ways of communicating and these are still being developed. You can not retract an e-mail once sent, it is there and it is accessible. Video conferencing may throw up different individuals as group leaders than the traditional meeting. It calls for different skills and makes it far more difficult to hold the floor, for example physical presence is less in evidence and you can not drown someone out.

## Review exercise

Discuss two ways in which new technological advances, such as e-mail and video conferencing, are likely to affect communication in the workplace.

## Summary

This chapter has examined the role of groups in the workplace. It looked at social identity theory and the way in which group identity affects our self-image. It then examined group formation and discussed Tuckman's stages of group formation and Feldman's model of organisational socialisation. It then progressed to consider decision making in groups, including the phenomena of risky shift and groupthink. Group cohesiveness and intergroup conflict were discussed. Teamwork and the processes of social facilitation and social loafing were discussed. Finally communication strategies were discussed with some speculation as to the effects of new technology in these areas.

## Further reading

Goffman, I. (1961) *Asylums*. Anchor books. Doubleday. One of the best studies of the effect of membership of a large organisation, such as a psychiatric hospital, on the behaviour of the individual.

Feldman, D.C. (1976) A contingency theory of socialisation, *Administrative Science Quarterly* 21, 433–52. A description of the process of work socialisation in a hospital setting.

# 7

# Leadership

 Introduction
Theories of leadership
Gender and leadership
Summary

## Introduction

Furnham (1997: 515) defines leadership as 'the process of influencing the behaviour of individuals or groups towards the achievement of organisational goals'. Most large organisations have a hierarchical structure with managers at the top and it is presumed that these managers will display leadership skills. Leadership is a topic which is much older than occupational psychology. The questions of who should be a leader and what qualities they should have, have taxed philosophers and politicians for thousands of years. Are leaders born or are they made by circumstances? Do people need leaders at all or would they be better without them?

One basic problem is the use of the term 'leadership'. It is unclear what we are talking about. Is it a prime minister, an army general, the captain of the rugby team or the supervisor on the shop floor? All of these are leaders but is it reasonable to use the same explanations to cover all their activities? Does Adolf Hitler share many common characteristics with Nelson Mandela?

## Theories of leadership

There are several different theories of leadership. The oldest is the great person or trait approach which assumes that leaders have **innate** characteristics. Historically it was often believed that leadership traits were inherited and that great leaders were therefore the products of birth. For example in Europe in the Middle Ages monarchs believed that they held their position by 'divine right'. By this they meant that they had been appointed by God and that they had either inherited the appropriate characteristics from their family or that God would endow them with these at the moment they were anointed and crowned. Early psychologists started from the point of listing the characteristics, or traits, that a great leader should have. A more recent approach was the behavioural one which suggested that the leader was the one who adopted the best strategy for a particular situation. Later theories suggested that leadership was a question of a match between the individual and a specific set of circumstances: the right person being in the right place at the right time. These approaches will now be discussed in more detail.

### *The trait or great 'person' approach*

The age of this approach is perhaps most apparent from its sexist label. Until very recently it was labelled the great 'man' approach. It fails to mention great women. Obviously there have been many such as Queen Elizabeth I, Joan of Arc, Marie Curie and Indira Ghandi. Much of the initial research was completed before 1940 and it assumed that there are specific physical and personality traits which are present in successful leaders and which differentiate leaders from other people. The trait approach presumed that these characteristics are innate, that is that they are biologically based, and are not the product of learning or experience. Inherited physical traits that this theory attributed to leaders were above average height, good health and physical attractiveness, while inherited personality characteristics included bravery, dominance, intelligence and talkativeness. The term 'charismatic' also often appeared.

## Commentary on the great 'person' approach

When attempts have been made to correlate these characteristics with known leaders they have not met with a great deal of success. If one approaches this from a purely anecdotal standpoint historical records tell us that Julius Caesar was a small, unattractive man who suffered from epilepsy and Winston Churchill was a short, stout, plain man who was known to suffer from depression. There is a tendency to attribute characteristics to individuals because the individuals are leaders and you may like to consider this further. Members of the British Royal Family have attained their positions by accident of birth or marriage. Are any of them great persons or do we attribute characteristics to them because of their position? Alternatively have they developed these characteristics because they, to quote Shakespeare, 'have greatness thrust upon them'? Stogdill (1974) completed a study of so-called great men and failed to establish any meaningful evidence of universal traits of greatness. Yuki (1981) attempted to discover whether any of the characteristics traditionally ascribed to great leaders could be found in biographical and other literature describing great men and women. He found only very weak correlations with above average intelligence, talkativeness, the need to be dominant and self-confidence. This indicates that any relationship is likely to be small, particularly when one looks at the methods of data collection which involved retrospective accounts of leaders. It is inevitable that these will emphasise leadership qualities and ignore others. Other traits failed to display any relationship.

Not surprisingly this approach is now unpopular with academic psychologists although it has many exponents within popular culture. For example tabloid newspapers suggest from time to time that countries could become great again if only the right leader were to emerge.

Describe a famous person, celebrity or politician and assess the extent to which their position in society can be attributed to innate personality traits and how much to our perception of their personality because of their position in society.

*Progress exercise*

## The behavioural approach

In contrast to the trait approach the behavioural approach claims that leadership is a product of the style that the leader adopts. The effectiveness of a leader depends not on who they are but on what they do. Leadership styles can therefore be adapted to the situation. This theory is based on research by Lewin *et al.* (1939) who trained youth leaders to use one of three leadership styles whilst supervising boys making theatrical masks, these were

- autocratic
- democratic
- laissez-faire.

The *autocratic* leader took an authoritarian approach. He told the boys what to do but did not give them a demonstration of what was expected. Whilst in the room he maintained a very formal atmosphere, was extremely strict and did not encourage the boys to ask questions.

The *democratic* leader maintained a much less formal atmosphere. He explained the task to the boys and gave them a demonstration of what was expected. He chatted to them whilst they worked and encouraged them to come for advice with difficulties. When they did so he worked with them to resolve the problem.

The *laissez-faire* leader remained detached from the group. The group was given the task to do and the leader's intervention was kept to a minimum. He appeared consistently disinterested in the boys' work and gave the impression that he was not bothered about the outcome of the activity.

The leaders were asked to use one style with one group, and then to use a different style with another group. They all adopted all three styles on different occasions. The boys responded to the style of leadership, not the individual. The autocratic group produced good output whilst the leader was present but morale in the group was low and when the leader was not present they worked less hard and became aggressive towards each other. The democratic group had high morale and good output whether the leader was present or absent. The laissez-faire group produced very little and also experienced low morale. In terms of popularity the boys rated the democratic leader as the best, followed by the laissez-faire leader and finally the autocrat. The suggestion was therefore made that democratic styles of leadership were superior because they produced both high productivity and worker satisfaction.

This research was highly influential but it is difficult to draw conclusions from it. The sample group were young boys engaged in a leisure activity, not adult workers. It is also not surprising that individuals in a society which places a very high value on democratic practices work best in a group which is supervised in this way. It would be interesting to see the experiment repeated with children who had been socialised into an autocratic society. While it does indicate that behaviour is more important than personality over a short period of time, it is unlikely that an individual would consistently be able to behave out of character. If this is the case then the personality tests described in Chapter 4 must have no value whatsoever!

### Task-orientated and socio-emotional leaders

Bales (1950) observed numerous groups where college students discussed a range of work-related problems in laboratory conditions, and they suggested that two types of leader emerged in such groups: **task-orientated** and **socio-emotional** leaders. Task-orientated leaders focus on completing a job and are not concerned with group interaction. Socio-emotional leaders are more concerned with the welfare of individuals in the group and with facilitating positive relationships within the group. One could state that the task-orientated leader has a masculine focus while the socio-emotional leader has a feminine one, a point which we will return to later in this chapter. This study has been criticised because it was based on observations of a group of college students in a laboratory setting and not a real life leadership situation. However when Halpin and Winer (1952) asked people to describe the behaviours which good leaders display and analysed the results they identified two main factors: showing consideration and initiating structures. A considerate leader displays concern for their subordinates and is interested in their welfare, an idea very close to that of the socio-emotional leader. The leader who initiates structures focuses on the task in hand and structures both their own role and the activities of the subordinates around the achievement of the group's objectives. This is similar to the task-orientated leader. Bales (1950) indicated that one individual could not undertake both functions and felt that two leaders are needed, one for each function. Stogdill (1974) indicated that the most effective leaders are those who can display both styles. Are the two positions conflicting or complementary? In some companies these two roles are separated, the production manager is task orientated and the human resources manager is socio-emotional in approach. Officer selection in the British Armed Forces looks for candidates who can offer both these qualities.

## The situational approach

The identification of different types of leadership qualities led to the suggestion that leaders emerge to meet the demands of the situation. McGregor (1960) suggested that the situation and not the individual's personality dictate leadership style. The great person theory suggests that there are universal personality traits of leadership, i.e. the same traits function the world over. The situational theory suggests that the force of circumstances may be much more powerful. An individual can become a leader if they find themselves in a highly favourable situation whilst another, with the qualities described in the great person approach, may fail as a leader in a situation which goes wrong because of factors completely beyond their control. You will be aware of football managers who have left one club as a great success and then failed miserably at the one that they moved on to. It is possible that something as simple as where one sits in a meeting affects the perception of leadership and qualities, and that taking the chair at the head of a table can confer leadership.

It may also be that the attitudes and beliefs of the individuals who are to be led can affect the perception of leadership. In the USA Rice (1980) looked at the reaction of army cadets at the West Point Academy. Cadets, who had previously been assessed as liberal or conservative in their outlook, were assigned to either a male or female group leader. Liberal-minded cadets felt that both male and female leaders were equally competent and skilful. However the conservative students felt that the male-led group succeeded because of a high level of co-operation and hard work in the group whilst the female success was put down to good luck. The conservative students were unwilling to attribute leadership characteristics to a woman, regardless of her performance, suggesting that gender may be a further situational determinant of the perception of leadership qualities.

### Fiedler's contingency theory

Fiedler (1967) developed the contingency theory. He suggested that the effectiveness of a leader depends, or is contingent upon, a good quality match between the leadership style of the individual, the characteristics of those who will be led and the favourability of the situation. He developed the concept of the 'least preferred co-worker' (LPC) to express this, basing his ideas on Bales's concepts of socio-emotional and task-orientated leaders. Leaders who have a high LPC score assess all their co-workers positively, even if they are very poor workers. The leaders show a preference for flexible working methods. Leaders who have a low LPC score distinguish between co-workers and rate them accordingly, being favourable to the good workers and unfavourable to those who they view as inefficient or poor workers. These leaders prefer a structured working environment. Low LPC leaders do well in situations which are either highly favourable or highly unfavourable. In highly favourable situations their attitudes are unlikely to have an effect as everyone will be happy. In highly unfavourable situations the completion of the task will override other issues. In situations which fall between these two extremes, personal feelings and issues may come to the fore and a high LPC leader will do well.

#### Commentary on Fiedler's contingency theory

Fiedler studied a wide range of groups and leaders, including sports people, retail managers, factory workers and scientists and the findings from these studies confirmed his theory. His theory is close to the great person approach in that it sees the leader's characteristics as being innate. It leaves little room for the more modern concept of pragmatism, that a successful leader will trim their sails to the prevailing wind, appearing in high LPC mode when appropriate and transferring to low LPC if the situation becomes dramatically unfavourable. Can the successful leader be all things to all people?

If we can return to Winston Churchill for a moment, the allied victory in World War II is credited, at least in part, to his leadership skills. The war could be described as a highly unfavourable situation. In his earlier political career Churchill had changed political parties, had been relegated to the sidelines of British politics after an unsuccessful spell in the cabinet and was seen as a maverick. Had people been asked in the 1930s whether they thought he had the potential to lead a political party, let alone a country, the consensus would probably have been that he did not. Similarly the British electorate voted him out of power by an overwhelming majority after the war when the major task ahead was seen to be reconstruction and reconciliation, a task which would call for a high LPC leader. However, during the war he was extremely successful and popular. One could say that he was the right person in the right place at the right time. However his reputation still varies geographically in the UK. A small boy who had moved to a Wiltshire school from the valleys of south Wales was asked who Churchill was. He replied instantly 'the man who shot the miners in Tonypandy'. An anecdote which perhaps says a lot about attribution of leadership qualities.

---

**Progress exercise**

When football teams are unsuccessful the usual reaction is to sack the manager and appoint another. The hope is that the new manager will have the personality and skills to ensure success and often teams do improve their performance initially.

Outline two reasons why a change of manager may cause an improvement in the team's performance. You may wish to consider trait or situational reasons. Remember that the club's owners may make more money available to buy new players and that the existing team members may try harder to avoid being transferred.

---

## Gender and leadership

In previous chapters the point has been made that much research on work and workers has been approached from a male perspective. Leadership is one such area. As stated, the great person theory was known as the great man theory until very recently.

Most organisations were based on the **patriarchal** model, that is they presumed that the natural order of things was that a man should be the leader. Armies consisted of and were led by men, a woman could only become the monarch if there was no male heir and the heads of most organised religions have been male. Women were not considered sensible enough to vote until the 1920s and the BBC did not have female newsreaders on television on the grounds that no one would believe them!

Women now make up over 40 per cent of the UK workforce but they hold only 20 per cent of management jobs in UK corporations and only 3.6 per cent of top executive positions (*Guardian* 1999). Do these differences reflect the relative suitability of males and females for management posts or not? If they do is it because males and females are biologically different or is it connected to the processes of socialisation? Referring back to Chapter 3 you will recall McClelland's nAch and the fact that he linked this characteristic to child-rearing styles. You may also recall the more recent work by Dweck which indicated that girls and boys receive different feedback about achievement. If successful leaders have a high nAch it may be that girls are socialised away from this style of behaviour before they enter the workplace.

Alternatively we may query the notion of nAch and other masculine traits, such as dominance and aggression, as an appropriate basis for leadership. In Chapter 1 we discussed the increasing feminisation of the workplace. If one examines the work of Bales it could be said that task-orientated leaders show male characteristics and socio-emotional leaders show female ones. If this is the case then maybe there are masculine and feminine leadership styles and one should appoint workers appropriately. More to the point should we be appointing managers who can use both styles successfully, regardless of their gender?

A third explanation is that women are quite capable of becoming managers but that they are prevented from doing so by stereotypes held by the existing male managers who are responsible for appointing them. If we refer back again to the section on interviews we see that people prefer to appoint others who are similar to them. One could argue therefore that a male would see a female as an inappropriate appointment because of both his view of the way the job should be done and because of his stereotype of female characteristics. The 'glass ceiling' again.

As for those who do succeed, Cockburn (1985) suggested that men appoint women who have a masculine style. Once the women are in post and in role they are then open to criticism for being unfeminine. Younger female colleagues are then discouraged, as it is perceived that success is incompatible with femininity. Whether one liked Margaret Thatcher or not this image does ring true!

Recent research reported in *The Observer* by the Pfaff human resources consultancy in Michigan, involving 2,500 managers in 240 companies in the USA, indicated that women used a wide range of management skills and were seen as equally competent to men in most areas and better in some.

**Review exercise**

Describe and evaluate one theory of leadership.

## Summary

This chapter has concerned itself with leadership and the development of theories over the twentieth century. The great person theory, which believes that particular personality traits are linked with leadership was introduced. This was followed by the behavioural approach, which takes the opposite view indicating that leadership is a question of adopting appropriate behavioural tactics. Bales introduced the idea that leaders could be task orientated or socio-emotional and more interested in personal welfare. The situational and contingency theories were then discussed. Both of these see leadership as a question of 'horses for courses'. Finally the question of gender and women leaders was introduced.

## Further reading

Hogg, M.A. and Vaughn, G.M. (1998) *Social Psychology* 2nd edn, Salisbury: Simon and Shuster. Chapter 8 presents a concise overview of the topic of leadership and also covers material on decision making which is relevant to Chapter 6 in this text.

# 8

# Study aids

## IMPROVING YOUR ESSAY WRITING SKILLS

At this point in the book you have acquired the knowledge necessary to tackle the exam itself. Answering exam questions is a skill, and in this chapter I hope to help you improve this skill. Examiners have first-hand knowledge about what goes wrong in exams. For example, candidates often do not answer the question which has been set, instead answering one that they had hoped would come up. Sometimes candidates do not make effective use of the knowledge they have but just 'dump their psychology' on the page in the hope that the answer is there somewhere. A grade C answer usually contains appropriate material but tends to be limited in detail and commentary. To lift such an answer to a grade A or B may require no more than a little more detail, better use of material and coherent organisation. It is important to appreciate that it may not involve writing at any greater length, it might even necessitate taking out some passages which do not add to the quality of the answer while elaborating those that do.

By studying the essays presented in this chapter and the examiner's comments, you can learn how to turn your grade C answers into grade As. Typically it only involves an extra 6 marks out of 30. Please note that marks given by the examiner in the practice essays should be used as a guide only and are not definitive.

You must provide the information that the examiner wants and not waste your time on irrelevant material. The answer will be marked out of 34 for OCR and 36 for Edexcel. Remember that these are the raw marks and are not equivalent to those given on the examination certificate received ultimately by the candidate because all examining boards are required to use a common standardised system, the Uniform Mark Scale (UMS) which adjusts all raw scores to a single standard acceptable to all examining boards. The questions from OCR and Edexcel are 'parted', that is divided into sections. It is important to read the question (this is not as obvious as it sounds). Each section will have a set number of marks. This is an indication of the amount of material required and you must pace your answer accordingly. If a section carries 10 marks then it requires more material than one which carries 6 marks.

The essays given here are notionally written by an 18-year-old in 30–40 minutes and are marked with this in mind. By studying them you should be able to tell the difference between an average and a good essay. It is important when writing to such a tight time limit that you make every sentence count. It is likely that the first section will require you to demonstrate what you have learned about the topic being examined, most students have acquired this type of skill at GCSE. Later sections will ask you to analyse and evaluate the material in the first section and to apply your knowledge to a practical situation. This is a more difficult skill to master but it will come with practice. Each essay in this chapter is followed by detailed comments about its strengths and weaknesses. The most common problems to watch out for are the following.

- Failure to answer the question set, giving instead a model answer to a similar question which you have pre-learned.
- Not delivering the right balance between description and evaluation. Remember for essay questions in this module both Edexcel and OCR marking schemes are weighted 40 per cent towards knowledge and understanding and 60 per cent towards analysis and evaluation.
- Writing 'everything you know' in the hope that something will get credit. Excellence demands selectivity, so improvements can be made by removing irrelevant material and elaborating material which is relevant to the question set.
- Failing to use your material effectively. It is not enough to place

the information on the page, you must also show the examiner that you are using it to make a particular point.

## Practice essay 1 (OCR)

### *Psychology and organisations*

Hi Ho, Hi Ho, it's off to work we go.

Why some people resent their jobs while others are enthusiastic about them, why some people look for additional work while others seem to avoid as much as they can, are questions which concern everyone interested in people's behaviour at work.

Blackler and Williams, 1971 (from an OCR paper)

Throughout history organisational psychologists have offered many theories of work motivation. Since the early days of Taylor (money and material incentives) and Mayo (interpersonal needs) more sophisticated theories have been developed, some emphasise specific needs while others focus on job design. Some propose cognitive theories of motivation and some view work outcomes as critical elements of worker motivation.

(a) Describe a number of theories of motivation in the workplace.

(8 marks)

(b) Evaluate these theories. (10 marks)

HINT: you may wish to consider the assumptions made about human behaviour, perspectives, for example need versus job design versus rational theories, how psychologists gained their evidence and the usefulness of the theories.

(c) Imagine that you are the personnel manager of a medium-sized law firm which employs a pool of about twenty typists, who are deployed on a daily basis to meet the needs of about fifty solicitors and legal executives. There are regular complaints from the legal staff about the poor quality of the typists' work and their tendency to 'clock watch'. Your records also indicate an excessively high staff turnover amongst typists. How might you intervene to improve the motivation of the typists in the pool? (6 marks)

HINT: indicate which theories of motivation you propose to apply.

*Starting point. Part (a) is worth 8 marks, one third of the total. It asks for a number of theories so do not spend all your effort describing only one. Also remember that the question asks for theories of motivation **in the workplace** so answer accordingly.*

*Part (b), which is worth 10 marks, asks you to evaluate the theories described in part (a) so do not introduce new ones. You could ask whether the theories are open to testing. Another issue is general-isability. Gender and cultural bias are present in many theories as many of them were constructed in the USA with reference to male, white-collar workers. Would they therefore be useful outside these settings and with other groups? They can also be said to represent a reductionist view of human beings, losing sight of the wider picture.*

*Part (c) which is worth 6 marks asks you to apply your knowledge to the problem of motivating individuals in a typing pool. There is no right answer here but you should tie any suggestions you make into basic theories. 'Giving them all a pay rise' may be a good idea but it will not get you many marks unless you explain why you would do this and what outcome you would expect!*

## Candidate's answer

(a) Several different theories of motivation are employed in the workplace: reinforcement theory, needs theory, cognitive theory, goal-setting theory, expectancy value theory and job design. These theories have been developed so that we can discover more about how people are motivated.

Reinforcement was a theory investigated by McGregor, Taylor and Herzberg. McGregor who researched and developed the theory X and theory Y idea believed that there were two causes of motivation. Theory X was when the managers employed the theory that workers are motivated due to conformity. They enjoyed following orders and carrying out menial tasks set by the manager. The theory Y manager believes that workers are motivated due to commitment to their jobs and their own personal self-esteem. Herzberg also held a similar 2-factor theory. He believed that workers were more motivated by intrinsic factors such as achievement, promotion, etc. than by extrinsic factors such as pay, safety and extra hours. Taylor held an opposing theory to this as he believed that money motivated individuals. Needs theory was something investigated by Maslow who invented a hierarchy of needs, believing that people were more motivated by self-actualisation than love and finally by safety. Alderfeld however disagreed with him, and said that people were influenced and motivated by their existence (safety), relatedness (love) and finally growth (self-actualisation).

The cognitive theory of motivation was held by Adams who believed that 'equity value theory' played an important role in motivation and that people's wages and salaries, etc. were not enough to motivate them. Whether or not their pay was the same as other workers mattered most.

Locke formed a goal-setting theory which has been proven to motivate people. The goals have to be small but of a suitable standard (not too easy). They also have to be personalised so that they relate to the individual. A sense of achievement is not felt when a goal has been completed if the goals are not specific but are too general. Feedback is essential in goal setting, as it helps the worker both by helping them (useful advice) and by motivating them (positive encouragement).

People are said to be motivated depending on the job and the reward – 'expectancy value theory'. Vroom suggested that people are motivated only if the task is worth doing for the size of the reward. Job design is essential in motivating a workforce. Taylorism (invented by Taylor) meant that workers were on a production line and performed one job all day. This was found to be ineffective as it was not a very humanistic approach. Hawthorne therefore formed the 'human relations' idea which meant that jobs were more personalised and workers had more say in the jobs they performed, and when they did them, etc. helping to motivate the workforce.

(b) Maslow's needs theory that self-actualisation is the most important method of motivation I find biased towards men. For women I feel that relatedness and love are more important than achievement. I also think that safety is more important than achievement. As shown in the Piliavin study on the train, subjects would only intervene and help the stooges if there was a low risk of them being hurt themselves. I therefore agree with Alderfeld more than Maslow.

It is true to a certain extent that Adams' 'equity value theory' is correct. People are motivated more by the way others are treated in comparison to themselves. An example of this is in-group and out-group discrimination in the Tajfel study. The boys were more inclined to reward the biggest difference in money that the groups got than to give the highest joint profit. Unfortunately this is human nature and it happens. This study was not however very ecologically valid, so I'm not sure of the validity of these results in an everyday situation.

Goal-setting theory is an essential part of motivation but can only take place if all four stages are carried out. Breaking down work into smaller components was an idea that Taylor had. He believed as Locke did that setting goals and specific targets helped to motivate a workforce. Taylor however took this to an extreme inventing 'fordism', the production line. Unfortunately this wasn't a humanistic approach and de-motivated workers having an adverse effect. Hawthorne however believed that responsibility and, as Herzberg described it, intrinsic control increased motivation.

He created the Volvo factory which embraced a new concept. Workers were designated a team who were responsible for making a whole car. This meant that workers had responsibility, and could also choose when they had breaks, what jobs they did, and gave them a more varied job. They did however still have goals which were set by the manager, for example how many cars should be made in a week. Although this was a more humanistic approach and motivated workers more it was found to be less cost effective and was therefore scrapped for the production line idea.

(c) Job design is essential to this type of work. Typists have minimal control over the amount of work they have and therefore are not motivated due to extrinsic factors. To improve motivation of the typists in the pool I would allow all twenty of them to decide to form a group. The management should then give them the freedom to make some of their own decisions such as how many days they work a week, etc.

It would help if the secretaries themselves could work out a rota giving them some responsibility. They could set themselves small daily targets or goals (goal-setting theory). The lawyers could also have a more friendly and sociable relationship with the typists so that they feel needed (Maslow's needs theory). They should make the typists feel that they are an essential part in the running of the business. Performance-related pay might also encourage the typists to work harder and maybe work for longer hours. They maybe should also be given more responsibility such as arranging meetings and appointments for the lawyers. It may be helpful if they each were responsible for two lawyers so that they had some control over the amount of paper work they get, so that it wasn't 'never ending'.

### Examiner's comments

*Part (a) is good because it covers a wide range of theories although some of them are not fully understood. The expression and structure are also unclear so it would not gain full marks, 6 marks out of 8.*

*The structure in part (b) is still muddled although it does stick to the theories used in part (a). There is misunderstanding in the interpretation of some of the theories, particularly Maslow and the information about the Volvo plant is not totally accurate. Whilst a candidate will not be penalised for mistakes they can not be credited for inaccuracies. Therefore this section reaches level two for analysis, evaluation and cross referencing but does not get into the higher mark band for structure, 6 marks out of 10*

*The final section is very good and shows that the candidate can apply his/her knowledge effectively to a real life situation. It comes up with a range of realistic options and links them into theories, 6 marks out of 6*

*Total marks 18 out of 24.*

### Practice essay 2 (OCR)

#### *A letter from America*

Dear Editor,

Recently I applied for a position and was told to expect an interview, followed by an assessment test. As they already had my CV, they had adequate evidence of my skills, qualifications and work history, so I told the personnel officer I was not interested in being subjected to the indignity of taking the 'assessment test'. She replied that it was merely intended to ensure that all employees were of the same standard, but her description of the test confirmed my suspicions that it was an American-style test which consisted of ridiculous questions and a choice of answers which have to be ranked in order of preference. The interviewer then interprets the results by consulting a list of numerals. Finally, the information could have been discerned by anyone taking the trouble to study the CV in the first place and conduct a proper interview.

A company which relies on tests to screen prospective employees isn't worth troubling with. They should stop wasting resources and insulting the intelligence of qualified people.

Mrs Chris Callingham

(a) Describe psychological evidence (theories and/or studies) relating to the selection of people for jobs. (8 marks)
(b) Evaluate psychological evidence relating to the selection of people for jobs. (10 marks)

HINT: your evaluation could include a discussion of the usefulness of the evidence; perspectives such as psychometric approach; the methods psychologists use to gain their evidence; the reliability and validity of testing.

(c) Based on the information you have presented, suggest how you, as a personnel officer, would select employees who will have to deal with the general public. (6 marks)

*Starting point. Part (a) asks the candidate to describe a range of both theories and research evidence. This is worth 8 of the available 24 marks and should therefore take up about one third of the answer. It would be easy to write far more than this and then have insufficient time to deal with the rest of the question.*

*Part (b) carries most marks (10). You are being asked to evaluate evidence only so do not be side-tracked into other areas. Concentrate on appropriate issues such as the validity and reliability of selection procedures and/or relevant research studies concerned with selection procedures, such as studies of interviewing. Part (c) asks you to apply your knowledge to a real-life problem and is worth 6 marks. This is central to OCR requirements and its aim is to ensure that you have understood the material studied and can apply it to a real-life situation. It requires you to think rather than regurgitate what you have learned. There are therefore no right answers here but you could discuss appropriate interviewing techniques or job analysis tasks. Make sure you apply your answer to the question.*

### Candidate's answer

(a)  Interviews, psychometric tests, biodata, references and 'in-tray' exercises can all be used to assess how suitable people will be for jobs. Interviews are the most traditional methods but, as shown by the study by Zanna and Copper, can sometimes not be a fair selection. They did an observation study using college students. A white interviewer interviewed black and white students and the interviews were observed using a two-way mirror and taped. The black candidates did not perform as well on the tasks in the interviews than the white candidates. The white candidates seemed more relaxed and conversation flowed much better.

Subsequently Zanna and Copper performed another study this time where the interviewers were trained thoroughly. The black and white candidates faired evenly on this test. This demonstrated that indirect discrimination was taking place in the interviews of the black candidates.

Psychometric tests are designed to test skills, personality and preferences. These however are quite controversial as many people are unwilling to take them because they are afraid that assessors may find out things about them that they didn't want them to know or that may not be true.

References are essential as they can prove what candidates are like in other situations, and maybe produce information that could not be identified over a short interview.

In-tray exercises are also vital as there is no point having a superbly qualified candidate who cannot do their job properly.

(b)  Methods and instruments used in selection should perform the following tasks:

- be fair so that there is no discrimination against age, sex, colour, etc.

- be reliable so that it is clear that the same results are obtained (no one has an unfair advantage)
- discriminate between candidates
- have valid results and actually show whether the candidate will be able to perform the job effectively
- they should not have an adverse impact on the client – deter them from applying for the job
- finally, they must be cost effective for the prospective employer.

Zanna and Copper showed that interviews can indirectly discriminate against some candidates and can be a poor method of selection without a sufficiently trained interviewer. They may also not be very fair as all interviews are different. They take up company time and resources and may not be very cost effective.

Psychometric tests are reliable as all candidates are given identical tests. They are however not very personalised, and do not allow subjects to express points of view, etc. They may also have an adverse impact on the applicants as they may be put off by the thought of a psychometric test. They are however quite cost effective because after producing one, it can be used over and over again. In-tray exercises are very good. They allow the candidates to perform, and the assessors to see what they are like in practice.

All of these methods however cannot be used on their own. It is essential because of their faults and strengths that more than one method is used to assess candidates.

(c) As a Personnel Officer selecting employees who will have to deal with the general public I would ensure that they had an interview. This would allow them to ask me any questions they had about the job, but would also allow me to find out about their personality. References would be essential (as many as possible) especially any relating to previous work in the field. I would also ask them to work on the job for a while, and even to do the menial tasks so that I could evaluate how they interacted with others. I am not really in favour of a psychometric test because they need to be able to interact with people as opposed to a piece of paper! They are a personnel manager, not a factory worker so social relations are essential.

***Examiner's comments***

*Part (a) lists a range of appropriate psychological evidence and therefore focuses well on the question's requirements. The study covered in depth (Zanna and Copper) has minor inaccuracies. The use of psychometric tests and in-tray exercises does not make it clear either what they are or what the purpose of using them would be, 6 marks out of 8.*

*Part (b) is very good and clearly states the purpose of using tests and then evaluates against these criteria, 6 marks out of 6.*

*Part (c) is the weakest part of the essay and does not do what is requested as it is not based on the evidence presented in any depth. It could have been written without any reference to the preceding sections, 3 marks out of 6.*

*Total marks 15 out of 24.*

## Practice Edexcel question 1

### *Topic D: the psychology of work*

Answer all *three* questions

*D1*

---

**Source One**

In view of the wide differences between jobs and between people it would be surprising if a group of applicants for a number of vacancies measured up completely and accurately to the psychological demand of the positions

Drenth and Algera in Warr, 1987, p. 113

---

Source One comments on the importance of personnel selection when considering the appropriateness of people for jobs.

(a) Outline *two* methods employed in selecting personnel.

(4 marks)

(b) Discuss the use of psychometric tests for recruitment of personnel. (8 marks)

(total 12 marks)

*D2*

---

**Source Two**

The group appears to be a rational creation: individuals come together, seek the best solution to a problem, and proceed to perform tasks to the best of their ability. Experience tells us, however, that such an ideal state does not always exist. Groups often make bad decisions.

Deaux and Wrightsman (from an OCR paper)

---

Source Two suggests that groups do not always make good decisions.

(a) Define group cohesiveness. (4 marks)
(b) Describe *two* factors affecting group decisions. (6 marks)
(c) Assess ways in which *two* factors affect group decisions. (6 marks)

(total 16 marks)

*D3*

---

**Source Three**

Three overlapping approaches to occupational stress may be identified, concerned primarily with the people's responses ('strain'), environmental features ('stressors'), or the interaction between stressors and responses through continuing processes of appraisal and coping.

Warr, 1987, p. 250

---

Source Three suggests that stress at work can come from the environment, the person or some interaction between the two.

(a)  Name *two* factors that produce stress at work.          (2 marks)
(b)  Assess ways in which *two* factors produce stress at work.

(6 marks)

(total 8 marks)

*Starting point. There will only be one question on the paper and it will be split into three sections as shown.*

*All three sources start with a requirement for Skill AO1 and ask for brief and accurate responses, the maximum mark asked for here is 4. The questions then move into more detailed requirements. All require you to apply your knowledge to practical situations and expect either accurate knowledge of appropriate psychological studies or relevant real-life evidence. Beware of anecdotal and generalised statements which may seem interesting but which will be marked for their psychological content or lack of content. For example, good use could be made of the concepts of validity and reliability for Source One and Source Three needs scientific evidence rather than journalistic generalisation.*

*Answer to Question 1*

D1 (a)  Outline *two* methods employed in selecting personnel.
Two methods employed are structured interviews and references. Structured interviews mean that the person wanting the job will be asked questions and they will be the same for everyone. References are statements about the applicant's previous work record and character. There may just be a form to fill in or they may be asked to write a report. Usually a previous employer or teacher will give them but it could be any responsible person. They help the employer to get another person's opinion of whether the candidate can do the job or not.

D1 (b)  Discuss the use of psychometric tests for the recruitment of personnel.
Psychometric tests are tests of ability. They can be used to see how good someone would be at a particular job or to measure intelligence or personality. They are standardised, that is tested on a group of people

**119**

before they are used. Psychometric tests must be valid and reliable. This means that they should measure what they say they are measuring and that a person's score must be the same if they do the test on different occasions.

Not all tests do this. It is possible for someone's score on an intelligence test to vary up to 15 points. With personality tests it may be that someone would lie and say what they thought the employer wanted rather than the truth because they want the job. Also some employers do not use the tests properly. They may have stocks of old tests around and use the wrong ones. This is because it is very expensive to employ a proper psychologist.

D2 (a) Define group cohesiveness.
Group cohesiveness means that a group will stick together. When people get together in a group they will all support each other because they feel part of the group.

D2 (b) Describe *two* factors affecting group decisions.
Two factors are Stoner's risky shift and Janis's groupthink. In the risky shift experiments people were asked to give odds on a decision on their own and then in groups. The decision could be whether someone left a secure job with poor wages for an insecure job which had very high wages. Stoner found that the group would take a higher risk than someone on their own. Janis studied decision making by politicians and people in the armed forces. He was interested in occasions when a group of people had made decisions which had bad consequences, such as Pearl Harbor and the Bay of Pigs. Afterwards everyone could see that they had made a mistake. He stated that there were pressures in groups which made them stop listening to other people and that once the group had decided on a course of action they believed it was right and would not change.

D2 (c) Assess ways in which *two* factors affect group decisions.
One factor is the need to conform to group expectations. Groups go through a stage known as norming when they make up group rules. Once this happens the people involved are supposed to stick to the rules. This means that it is difficult to speak out if you know the group is wrong and this is what happens in groupthink. One good way of studying group decisions is to look at decisions made by juries. Kerr

and Bray showed that juries were less likely to convict people if the penalty was very severe and Michelini showed that attractive defendants were less likely than unattractive defendants to be found guilty. This means that the juries were allowing things other than the evidence to influence their views.

D3 (a)  Name *two* factors that produce stress at work.

Factors that produce stress at work can be physical or psychological. Working night shift can be stressful because the person is working against their normal bodily rhythm. Uncertainty, not knowing what you have to do next or how long you have to do it can also be stressful because the person worries all the time about whether they are doing the right thing or not.

D3 (b)  Assess ways in which *two* factors produce stress at work.

Working shifts is stressful because your body has a natural 24-hour rhythm called a circadian rhythm. This means that you would normally sleep at night and be awake in the day. If you are on night shift then you are awake at night and this has been shown to cause problems. Cziesler did a study in the USA where people were changing shift every week and working backwards. He changed the schedule to every 3 weeks and made it follow the clock. The workers were less stressed and healthier. Hawkins studied nurses and showed that there were differences between individuals and that some people are more stressed by night-working than others. People such as social workers and nurses in casualty units are said to have high stress rates. This is because they do not know what will happen next. For example drunks in casualty units may become violent. Also there may not be enough beds for people and they have to keep them on trolleys in corridors. Both these things are stressful and people working in these settings sometimes suffer from burnout.

### Examiner's comments

*This student has worked hard and learned appropriate material but has failed to make the best use of it. Whilst the description (AO1) is accurate the attempts to analyse and evaluate (AO2) are limited and not applied to the work situation or (sometimes) to the point of the question.*

*D1 (a) 4 marks out of 4. The student has correctly identified and outlined two methods of selecting personnel.*

*D1 (b) 5 marks out of 8. This answer is in insufficient detail. The definition of psychometric tests is inadequate. The student gains marks for raising the issues of standardisation, validity and reliability but fails to make adequate use of these points. The evaluative statements are too general and specific research is not quoted. Also this section is not much longer than the previous one. While you will not be marked on the basis of length there is a relationship between marks and examiner's expectations.*

*D2 (a) 2 marks out of 4. There is insufficient material here for 4 marks. The material is accurate and pertinent but does not explain the concept of cohesiveness fully. It may be useful to compare it to the amount of material in D1 (a).*

*D2 (b) 4 marks out of 6. Two factors affecting group decisions are correctly identified and appropriate research quoted. However the understanding shown is limited and the language used shows a poor use of psychological terminology. The answer reads more like a GCSE response than the standard expected for A-level year 2.*

*D2 (c) 3 marks out of 6. This last section is much too brief. Neither concept is explained clearly and the answer consists of description of the way factors affect decisions rather than assessment. Much better use could have been made of the material on the behaviour of Jurors.*

*D3 (a) 2 marks out of 2. The student has full marks here but has done more than was required. They have not merely named two factors which produce stress but have expanded unnecessarily. There is much more here for two marks than there was for four in D2.*

*D3 (b) 4 marks out of 6. This section attempts to answer the question and the section on shift working is quite good as it uses psychological terminology and appropriate research to illustrate the point. However the section on unpredictability and burnout is less clear. It quotes anecdotal evidence but fails to apply it to the question properly. Why do the nurses in casualty units feel stress and suffer from burnout? There should be material on control and the consequences of working in such an unpredictable environment. What is burnout?*

*Total marks: 24 out of 36, Grade C.*

## Practice Edexcel question 2

### *Topic D: the psychology of work*

Answer all *three* questions

D1

---

**Source One**

There are major problems in measuring job motivation. Asking people is problematic, both because people find it very difficult to report their motives accurately . . . as well as the fact that there are strong pressures put on people to give socially desirable, rather than truthful, answers.

Furnham, 1997, p. 293

---

Source One comments on the difficulties involved in assessing a candidate's level of motivation for employment or promotion.

(a) Describe *one* theory of motivation at work.                    (5 marks)
(b) Discuss *two* types of psychometric tests which could be used in selecting individuals for promotion at work.                    (7 marks)

(total 12 marks)

D2

---

**Source Two**

Leaders behave differently, or so the theory goes, otherwise they would not be the leader. What is it about their behaviour that makes them suitable to lead?

Porteous, 1997, p. 274

---

Source Two suggests that leaders may be different to other people.

(a) Define autocratic and democratic styles of leadership. (2 marks)

(b) Outline *two* factors which affect decision making in groups.

(4 marks)

(c) Discuss *one* theory of leadership effectiveness. (6 marks)

(total 12 marks)

*D3*

---

**Source Three**

An important footnote to any discussion of work and stress is the issue of unemployment and stress . . . we can see that unemployment brings its own stresses . . . Unemployed people have a very ambiguous role, and they do not get support from relationships at work.

Banyard, 1996, p. 146

---

Source Three suggests that both employment and unemployment can be stressful.

(a) What do psychologist mean by the term stress? (2 marks)

(b) Outline *two* factors which produce stress at work. (4 marks)

(c) Assess the psychological effects of unemployment
for the individual. (6 marks)

(total 12 marks)

*Starting point. Source One asks for any theory of motivation at work and the answer, which is worth 6 marks, should be longer than a definition and it should include detail. Be careful with part (b) of Source One as you are being asked to apply your answers to selecting individuals for promotion. A general answer on psychometric tests will not gain full marks. Source Two is concerned with leadership and groups. Keep your sections separate as required. Again it is the last section which asks for Skill AO2. Source Three asks for knowledge of stress at work (AO1) but asks the candidate to **assess** the effects of unemployment on the individual. It would be sensible therefore to look at unemployment as a stressful event.*

D1 (a)  Describe *one* theory of motivation at work.

Herzberg's theory suggested that there were two sets of needs in the workplace, hygiene needs and motivator needs. Hygiene needs include external factors such as the salary for the job and a safe, clean and secure working environment. Herzberg stated that the absence of these factors would create dissatisfaction and that the workers would therefore not perform efficiently. Motivator needs are intrinsic and would include the ability to use skills and be given personal credit for this, opportunities for growth such as further training and being given responsibility for organising one's own and possibly other people's workloads. Herzberg stated that both sets of needs should be met to produce a highly motivated workforce. A high salary on its own would not necessarily compensate for a dangerous environment, although workers may be paid extra for 'dirty jobs'. Similarly one may not take up a job where one's skills may be appreciated and one was given freedom of creative expression if the wages were very poor.

D1 (b)  Discuss *two* types of psychometric tests which could be used in selecting individuals for promotion at work.

If someone is being considered for promotion at work one would presume that they are already competent in their present job. Appropriate psychometric tests should therefore have good predictive validity, which means that they should accurately measure performance in the skills that will be used in the new job. Two types of tests which could be used are intelligence tests and personality tests.

There are a range of different intelligence tests available and the company should choose one which is assessing appropriate areas of intellectual ability. All the tests claim to measure intellectual ability. One presumes that employers would look for an above-average score in someone who is to be promoted. In fact the correlation between a high IQ score and effective performance as a manager is low. Those who score highest on such tests do not always make the best managers because many tests measure academic ability rather than expertise in a job, decision-making skills or effectiveness in dealing with people.

Personality tests are based on the idea that each individual has a number of stable characteristics or traits which can be measured, usually by filling in a questionnaire. The employer would definitely need to choose the correct test as the promotion may require characteristics which have not yet been displayed. However if candidates know what characteristics are being requested they might complete their form accordingly. It is also difficult to know whether scores predict future performance or reflect past skills. Sales staff usually score highly for extroversion on personality tests. Is this because extroverts make good sales people or because a period in sales develops the extravert side of your personality? The purpose of both kinds of tests is to assist in selection processes and Porteous, who has reviewed a number of pieces of research in this area, states that they are as efficient as other methods and superior to many.

D2 (a)  Define autocratic and democratic styles of leadership.
These terms were used by Lewin *et al.* in a study of leadership over 50 years ago. Autocratic leaders are very controlling, use a very strict regime and behave in a formal manner. They control rather than guide. Democratic leaders guide rather than control. They explain tasks, make sure everyone understands the task they are working on and allow autonomy to each individual. They will be friendly to those in their group and less distant than autocratic leaders.

D2 (b)  Outline *two* factors which affect decision making in groups.
Two factors which could affect decision making in groups would be groupthink and the risky shift. Groupthink, described by Janis, is the tendency of highly cohesive groups who wish to make a unanimous decision to avoid normal procedures and adopt strategies which may turn out to be very foolish. The members of the group become convinced that they are right (invulnerability) and reject any views which do not agree with theirs, either by discounting the view or by negatively stereotyping the source of the opinion. The risky shift phenomenon was described by Stoner. When faced with a dilemma which involved an individual making risky choices about their future, groups were willing to give longer odds than individuals, indicating that a group would be less cautious in decision making than individuals.

D2 (c)  Discuss *one* theory of leadership effectiveness.
Fiedler's theory suggests that effective leadership is contingent on a match between the personality of the leader and the nature of the task. He developed the LPC (least preferred co-worker) scale which

measures the leader's attitude towards their colleagues. His work was based on Bales's concepts of task-orientated and socio-emotional leaders. High scorers on the scale were positive towards their fellow workers and low scorers were negative. Fiedler suggested that low LPC scorers would do best in highly favourable or unfavourable conditions and high LPC scorers in middle-range conditions. The theory can be criticised. It presumes that leadership styles are consistent, when there are indications that successful leaders are able to vary their style to suit the situation and it takes no account of the behaviour and attitudes of followers.

D3 (a)  What do psychologists mean by the term stress?

When psychologists use the term stress they are using a term borrowed from physics. They are describing the ways in which an individual responds to pressures from the environment. A certain amount of stress may be good as it can strengthen the individual but too much can be harmful.

D3 (b)  Outline *two* factors which produce stress at work.

Job insecurity means that the individual will be uncertain about their future and feel that the situation is beyond their control. Lack of control in one's life has been identified as a major source of stress. Depending on the economic state of the country and their age the individual may be uncertain of getting another job at all or may fear that they will have to take one which offers a much lower standard of living. They may have to relocate to find a job.

Role ambiguity occurs when conflicting demands are placed on workers, either by different parts of the organisation or by a conflict between the demands of work and their home life. A good illustration of role ambiguity would be the conflicting demands of a high-powered job and one's responsibility as a parent. If extra demands are made at work and a child is sick then the individual would experience conflict about prioritising these demands.

D3 (c)  Assess the psychological effects of unemployment for the individual.

Unemployment has consistently been shown to have deleterious effects in western industrialised countries over the last 70 years. Jahoda's studies in the 1930s showed that the effects increased as the period of unemployment lengthened, stating that the long-term unemployed were likely to suffer from apathy and depression. Warr claims that work provides both financial and psychological security. Losing one's job means uncertainty about one's place in society as well as loss of income, and he refers to this as lack of environmental clarity. Beale, in the 1980s, showed that people's health was affected from the point they received the redundancy notice, that is before they actually experienced the unemployment. He compared the health of those made redundant to a group of matched individuals who stayed in employment and showed that rates of chronic illness increased and that there was a sixfold increase in referrals to hospital specialists compared to the control group. These studies show a link between unemployment and poor physical and psychological health. However most studies have concentrated on male employees and there is uncertainty about the effect of unemployment on women, although they fared worse than the men in the Beale study. It may also be that unemployment has different effects at different points in a person's life and that for some people, such as those with a chronic illness which may be aggravated by their working environment, unemployment may actually improve their overall health. To conclude, unemployment usually has a bad effect on people but there will be individual differences, as there are in all areas of psychology.

### Examiner's comments

*This student has made much more effective use of the material they have learned and has kept to the rubric of the questions. The answers are accurate, detailed and well structured (AO1) and a good level of critical understanding is displayed (AO2). The candidate has also applied answers to the working situation where this is appropriate (AO2).*

*D1 (a) 4 marks out of 5. The candidate has covered the area fairly well. Herzberg's theory is correctly identified and described, however the assessment and evaluation of the theory could be more detailed.*

*D1 (b) 6 marks out of 7. Two types of tests are identified and described correctly. There is effective evaluation of both positive and negative studies and opinions on the tests, and an indication of why they would be appropriate as tests for promotion.*

*D2 (a) 2 marks out of 2. Clear, accurate and concise definitions.*

*D2 (b) 4 marks out of 4. Two factors are accurately identified and outlined. Compare this answer with the one given for D2 (b) in Question 1 to illustrate the difference between an average and a very good mark.*

*D2 (c) 5 marks out of 6. An appropriate theory is produced and described but the discussion is insufficiently detailed for 6 marks.*

*D3 (a) 2 marks out of 2. Accurate enough to get 2 marks but it could be clearer.*

*D3 (b) 3 marks out of 4. Two stress factors are correctly identified. The answer does veer towards the journalistic and 1 mark is lost for lack of hard psychological content. Much of this could have been written by a candidate with good general knowledge.*

*D3 (c) 5 marks out of 6. A well-written response which describes appropriate psychological evidence of the effects of unemployment but which could make more detailed use made of Warr's studies for assessment purposes. However the final two sentences draw the material together nicely.*

*Total marks 33 out of 36, Grade A.*

## KEY RESEARCH SUMMARIES

### Article 1

**Beale, N. and Nethercott, S. (1985) Job loss and family morbidity: a study of factory closure, *Journal of the Royal College of General Practitioners* 35, 510–14.**

*Introduction*

In western societies where there is full employment there has been concern about the psychological and physiological effects of unemployment. This is a naturalistic experiment study completed by a general practitioner (GP), examining the medical records of patients who were made redundant by the closure of a food-processing factory.

*Background*

After a period of relative prosperity unemployment began to escalate in the UK during the 1970s and 1980s. Work by Jahoda in the 1930s had indicated that there were links between spells of unemployment lasting 6 months or more and psychological well-being. There have been other, more recent, studies by Warr *et al.* showing links between unemployment and physical illness. Calne is a small town in the south of England, situated not far from Swindon. The main employer in the town was the Harris food-processing factory. This factory had been established in the town for many years and several families had a three-generation history of working in the plant. The factory closure was well heralded and many employees had 2 years' notice of job loss. This presented the local GP with the opportunity to examine the effects of unemployment on a stable workforce, which had both male and female employees. Most research until then had concentrated on the effects of unemployment on males.

## Research aims

To examine the effects of unemployment on mental and physical well-being by measuring referrals for GP consultations and subsequent referrals to consultants and specialists.

## Method

The GP was interested in the impact that the closure of the factory belonging to the main employer in the town would have and speculated that there might be a decrease in referrals with less industrial accidents and related illnesses. He therefore worked with a statistician using the situation as a naturalistic experiment. The redundant workers were matched with employed individuals and the health records of the two groups compared by extracting details from the medical records of both groups over a period of years, commencing at the point when the redundancy notices were first issued. In this way it was hoped that any differences in the health of the two groups would be a consequence of unemployment and that other variables would be eliminated. In common with many other west country towns Calne has a mix of individuals working locally, often in low-paid employment and wealthier commuting workers who travel to Swindon or to greater London daily. It was important to use workers with similar backgrounds and the matching was therefore done very carefully.

### Results

The results showed a significant difference between the health of the two groups, with redundancy having a greater effect on female workers. This difference was evident from the point at which the redundancy notices were issued and not the point when the unemployment started. This gap sometimes extended to 2 years. The number of visits to the doctor's surgery increased from the point at which the redundancy notices were issued, and the number of patients referred to a specialist was six times higher in the unemployed workers than in the control group. The illnesses were long-term physical conditions such as asthma, arthritis and high blood pressure, as well as psychological conditions such as depression and anxiety-related disorders.

### Discussion

This research shows a clear link between unemployment and health. The effect would appear to be linked to the perception of the situation as much as the actual experience of unemployment. The researchers initially believed that the unemployment had failed to have an effect as they measured changes occurring after the actual redundancy. It was only when they back tracked a further 2 years to the issuing of the redundancy notices that the effects became clear. This research was also one of the first to indicate that the effects of redundancy could be as severe for women employees as for men. It may be difficult to generalise from the research as Calne was dominated by this employer and the effects may therefore have been particularly damaging as the closure of the factory had wide-reaching effects in the community. However this did not affect the control group.

### Questions for discussion

1. Why was it important to use a matched participants design with this survey?
2. What does the study tell us about the point at which unemployment takes effect?

## Article 2

### Janis, I.L. (1982) Groupthink

#### Introduction

Efficient decision making in organisations is central to their productivity. It is usual for groups to be involved in making major decisions and psychologists are interested in how groups form and function. Janis attempted to match psychological theory with historical events.

#### Background

In 1961 the USA, led by President J.F. Kennedy, embarked on a disastrous attempt to invade Cuba. Not only was the invasion a failure, leading to worldwide condemnation and ridicule for the USA, but it also strengthened the position of Fidel Castro, the Cuban president, when the main aim had been to undermine him. As this kind of embarrassing fiasco had precedents, for example Pearl Harbor and the Vietnam War, Janis used the existing work on group dynamics from Kurt Lewin and other American social psychologists to explore the decision-making processes involved. He examined the records from hundreds of relevant documents and coined the name 'groupthink' for the process involved.

#### Research aim

To identify the processes which occur in groups and lead to decisions which later cause comments such as J. F. Kennedy's 'How could we have been so stupid?' To examine whether decisions occur because of the individuals involved or because of processes occurring in the group.

#### Method

The method involved was content analysis, using secondary data by studying documentation from official records, media reports and subsequent autobiographical details from individuals involved in the Bay of Pigs scandal and several other American miscalculations, including the war in Vietnam. Documents from successful group decisions, such as the Marshall plan, which gave financial aid to Europe after World War II, were also examined.

### Findings

Janis attempted to explain the psychological processes that occur in groups and described a number of factors which he believed must be present for groupthink to occur.

1. *Invulnerability* the group ignores warning signals, become impulsive and takes high risks.
2. *Rationale* the group ignores information that disagrees with or undermines their position.
3. *Morality* the group members believe that they are right and that their solution is morally correct. They view those who disagree with them or obstruct them as evil.
4. *Stereotypes* the group adopts a negative view of opposing views and therefore refuses to take other opinions seriously.
5. *Pressure* anyone who expresses doubts inside the group is viewed as disloyal and may be required to leave the group.
6. *Self-censorship* individuals who do discover material which may undermine the agreed position are likely to suppress it rather than cause disagreement.
7. *Unanimity* members of the group will reinforce each other's position and encourage the belief that everyone is in constant agreement.
8. *Mindguards* the group members protect each other from contamination by negative information which may undermine their position.

Janis made recommendations for good group practice in order to avoid groupthink.

### Discussion

The article was highly influential and its main recommendations are still important in the organisation of governmental and industrial decision making in western societies. The group may use disinterested outsiders or experts to guide and advise them or appoint an individual in the group to play the 'devil's advocate' and to deliberately take up a critical position. Alternatively the group members may delegate parts of the decision-making process to others. As an example the UK parliament makes extensive use of select committees which have cross-party membership and whose role is to analyse and criticise proposed legislation. However Janis's findings are subjective and based on analysis after the event when everyone is attempting to explain what happened! The study's findings are also culture bound in that they describe decision making in the USA and may only apply to western, democratic settings.

### Questions for discussion

1. Describe a more recent example of groupthink and use Janis's list of factors to explain what took place.
2. Draw up a list of rules for committee functioning which you think would prevent groupthink.

## Article 3

### The Whitehall studies

**Marmot, M.G. and Rose, E. (1981) Social class and coronary heart disease, *British Medical Journal 45*, 13–19.**

#### Introduction

The relationship between employment status and health has been a point of discussion in both organisational psychology and the health service. The traditional view, prior to the 1960s, was that managers' jobs are more stressful than those of lower grade workers as they had executive responsibilities, such as making decisions, which affected the lives of others. It was therefore presumed that they were more at risk of stress-related illnesses. The risks for low-status and unskilled workers were considered to be physical and not emotional. This survey aimed to re-examine this idea and to look at the relationship between employment status and stress-related illness in a white-collar setting.

#### Background

During the 1960s the differential mortality rates between occupational groups became increasingly apparent. It was, however, considered that the higher mortality rates in lower social groups were due to physical dangers and hazards in the working environment. Marmot and Rose investigated health and mortality rates in white-collar workers by completing surveys and tracking the health records of a large number of London-based civil servants, a group that tends to have stable employment patterns and few obvious hazards in the work environment. It was therefore felt that any differences in health patterns could be related to psychological factors in the working environment. It was hypothesised that the inability to make decisions and to control workload could be as damaging as taking executive responsibilities. All civil servants are employed on a specific grade which clearly indicates their level of responsibility. They have a medical when they start work and good records of their health are kept throughout their period of employment. Relevant data was therefore available for study.

### Research aim

To examine the relationship between employment grades and health and mortality rates in civil servants. Marmot and Rose wanted to discover which types of job created most stress and they felt that this could be measured by examining the incidence of stress-related and other illnesses in a workforce which had a range of different types of jobs.

### Method

A longtitudinal survey and correlational study used the employment and health records of 17,000 civil servants to examine mortality rates and the incidence of serious illness. Surveys were conducted into the eating habits and leisure activities, for example exercising and smoking and drinking rates among the participants. Follow-up questionnaires and clinical examinations were completed between 1985 and 1988 to check the findings further.

### Results

The study displayed a negative relationship between employment grade and health: the lower the grade of civil servant the higher the mortality rate and the greater the incidence of most serious illnesses. The

**135**

incidence of stress-related illnesses such as coronary heart disease, ulcers and cancers was higher in lower grade workers than in those on higher grades. Those in the lowest grade had a mortality rate three times higher than those in the highest. These findings were true regardless of the health of the workers when they commenced employment, eliminating the possibility that workers in poor health were allocated to low-grade jobs. Data revealed that the lower grade workers perceived that their health was poorer, took less exercise and had poorer diets, 61 per cent of this group were heavy smokers in contrast with the higher grades where the rate was 29 per cent.

The follow-up survey also showed similar results. Clinical examinations showed higher rates of angina, electrocardiograph evidence of ischemia and symptoms of chronic bronchitis in the lower status groups when they were compared with the higher grades.

## Discussion

The results suggest a link between employment status and health. Marmot and Rose suggested that the fact that the lowest grade workers had low status and had little control over either their type of work or the work rate expected of them caused their poor health. Making decisions indicates that you are in control. Not being able to make decisions about the type of work one does or the pace at which it should be done indicates a lack of control. Powerlessness may possibly be a cause of stress-related illness.

However it is evident that the lower grade workers had less healthy life styles and it is difficult to disentangle the effects of work and home life. Low-grade civil servants are very poorly paid and possibly less able to afford a healthy diet or to take part in healthy leisure activities. These differences in life style may be financial or cultural. For example smoking may be viewed as an acceptable method of relieving stress. It is difficult to separate cause and effect.

## Questions for discussion

1. Why is it important that white-collar workers were used in this study?
2. What could one conclude about the effects of stress in the workplace? Is the role of a chief executive more or less stressful

than that of a poorly paid unskilled worker? What different stresses may be involved in the two jobs?
3. What other factors in the workers' lives may have contributed to the differences in the health and mortality rates?

# Glossary

**adaptive response** a response which increases the individual's potential to survive. A tactic which will enable the individual to be successful in avoiding or escaping from threat.

**additional decrement** see **determinants**.

**aesthetic needs** the need for creative stimulation and expression. Part of Maslow's hierarchy.

**anxiety** a state of worry, apprehension and possibly fear occasioned by the perception of a threat to the individual. It is usually accompanied by physiological reactions such as rapid heart beat, sweating and stomach tightness.

**attitude** a favourable or unfavourable response to a person, situation or object. Attitudes are said to be held at cognitive (thinking), emotional (feeling) and behavioural levels.

**attribution** the process of inferring the causes of another person's behaviour and/or attitudes.

**behaviourism** an approach to psychology that states that all behaviour is acquired through the processes of classical and operant conditioning. For behaviourists it is only worth measuring actions or behaviours. Cognitive processes can not be measured and it is therefore inappropriate to study them.

**biodata** biographical data. The collection of the personal history and details of both successful and unsuccessful employees. This data is then used as a tool to select future employees, based on the idea that those who fail and succeed in the future will have similar characteristics to those who have failed or succeeded in the past.

**blue-collar** a term originating in the USA used to describe manual workers.

**burnout** mental and/or physical exhaustion caused either by overwork or by stress at work.

**classical conditioning** learning by association. One stimulus is consistently followed by another and the individual learns to predict stimulus two from the occurrence of stimulus one. Classical conditioning was first described by Pavlov.

**cognitive needs** the need for intellectual stimulation and fulfilment. Part of Maslow's hierarchy.

**conditioning** the acquisition of behaviour by the processes of operant and classical conditioning.

**constant effect** see **determinants**.

**curriculum vitae** literally the route of life. A biographical résumé that includes personal details, qualifications and work experience, that will be presented to an employer by a job seeker.

**demographic details** factors such as age, sex and marital status.

**determinants** a concept used by P. Warr. Factors which are essential for the individual's psychological well-being.

**constant effect** determinants whose presence is essential. A minimum level is essential and large amounts have no undesirable effects.

**additional decrement** determinants which can be harmful if they are present in excess.

**environmental clarity** the extent to which the individual is familiar with, understands and feels in control of events.

**esteem needs** the need for status in a group and respect from one's fellows. Part of Maslow's hierarchy.

**extrinsic** in terms of motivation the use of external factors to motivate and control a person's behaviour.

**extrovert** see **introvert**. A personality dimension initially described by Jung and later used by Eysenck. Extroverts are sociable, outgoing and gregarious. They are said to be difficult to condition and have low anxiety levels.

**face validity** see **validity**

**facilitation** the process of making things easier. In social psychology the term is used to describe the process by which an individual's performance improves in the presence of others.

**feminisation** occupations are said to be feminised when women join them in significant numbers.

**fundamental attribution error** the tendency to explain an individual's behaviour in terms of their personal characteristics rather than social influences. It presumes that an individual will overestimate the former and underestimate the latter when judging someone else.

**group** a small number of individuals who share a common purpose.

**growth needs** the need for intellectual and creative stimulation and opportunity. Part of Maslow's hierarchy of needs.

**groupthink** decision making which takes place in highly cohesive groups. A consensus is formed, often by suppressing conflicting information, resulting in incorrect decisions.

**human resources department** the section or department in an organisation which deals with areas of staffing such as selection, training and welfare. These departments were previously known as personnel departments.

**humanist** a psychological approach which is centred on the individual. It emphasises the unique nature and life experience of each person and believes that each person's subjective experience is central in their understanding and interpretation of their own behaviour.

**hygiene needs** needs that arise from conditions that occur in the workplace (see Herzberg's two-factor theory, p. 36).

**industrial psychology** see **organisational psychology**.

**inhibition** the process of making things difficult. In social psychology the term is used to describe the process by which the presence of others detracts from an individual's performance and makes them less competent.

**innate** innate behaviour is not learned. Innate behaviours are part of the individual's genetic makeup.

**intelligence tests** intelligence is the ability to learn efficiently, to profit from experience and to deal effectively with one's environment. Testing intelligence is presumed to indicate an individual's level of functioning in these areas.

**intrinsic** in terms of motivation intrinsic relates to the role of internal factors in the organisation and control of a person's behaviour.

**introvert** see **extrovert**. Introverts are shy and cautious, they enjoy their own company and avoid noisy environments. They are said to be easy to condition and have high levels of anxiety.

**job analysis** the process of collecting information to produce an accurate description of a job. It is usually done before the selection of employees for a job.

**job specification** the description of a job. It is usually compiled as a result of job analysis.

**karoshi** a Japanese term referring to overwork as a cause of death.

**life event** an occurrence in the individual's life that is acknowledged to be an important milestone. A point of transition that is acknowledged by wider society.

**meta analysis** analysis based on data collected from a number of studies.

**motivation** the forces that direct behaviour. An individual is said to be motivated when they are seeking to fulfil a need.

**motivator needs** needs that arise from the desire for personal satisfaction, opportunities for advancement and professional growth and development (see Herzberg's-two factor theory, p. 36).

**nAch** the need for achievement. An individual with a high nAch would have a great desire to succeed.

**occupational psychology** the branch of psychology that deals with personal interactions in the workplace. This includes large and small companies and other organisations such as the armed forces and sports teams.

**operant conditioning** learning as a consequence of producing a behaviour. If an action is followed by a pleasant consequence it is likely to be repeated and added to the individual's repertoire of behaviour. If the action produces no outcome or is followed by an unpleasant consequence it is likely to stop.

**organisational psychology** see **occupational psychology**.

**patriarchy** the dominance of males over females. The term comes from Victorian households where the father was the head of the household and made all the rules. The women and children were subject to his rules.

**personal identity** that part of the sense of self which is based on the individual's personal characteristics.

**personality tests** tests which have been designed to measure personality traits in the individual.

**person specification** the description of the knowledge, skills and attitudes which an individual should possess to perform a particular job.

**personnel department** see **human resources department**.

**physiological needs** basic needs for survival such as food, water and shelter. Part of Maslow's hierarchy of needs.

**predictive validity** see **validity**

**primacy effects** the theory that the first item in a list or sequence will have a greater effect than later items.

**projective tests** unstructured psychological tests that allow a range of responses.

**psychodynamic** an approach to psychology which is based on Freudian theory. It emphasises the role of early childhood experiences and unconscious mental processes in determining behaviour.

**psychometric testing** the use of psychologically designed materials to select individuals for employment and training. Tests may cover a wide range of aptitudes from general intelligence to job specific skills.

**reliability** the consistency of test results over time. For a test to be reliable the scores should be the same or very similar on test and retest.

**risky shift** a theory, described by Stoner, that states that, following discussion, a group will move towards greater risk taking than each individual has proposed earlier.

**role conflict** conflict which occurs when an individual experiences differing demands from two or more roles in their life, such as paid work and domestic duties.

**safety needs** the need for physical and psychological security. Part of Maslow's hierarchy of needs.

**self-actualisation** a concept used by Maslow to refer to an individual's tendency to achieve their full potential.

**social identity** that part of the sense of self that is based on the groups with whom the individual has a relationship or connection.

**social learning theory** a theory of learning that involves learning by observing another individual and copying their actions.

**social loafing** the idea that individuals put in less effort when engaged as a group than they do when working alone.

**social needs** the need for the company and companionship of others. Part of Maslow's hierarchy of needs.

**socio-emotional** a style of leadership where the leader's priority is interpersonal relationships in the group rather than the completion of the task in hand.

**source traits** basic traits or characteristics which form the core or centre of an individual's personality.

**stereotypes** simple, fixed and inflexible views about an individual, group or set of ideas. Stereotypes can be useful in making rapid initial assessments but can also be counter-productive if they are negative.

**stress** literally a pressure or force exerted on an object. The emotional state which occurs when an individual believes that they do not have the resources to deal with a situation or series of events.

**structured interview** an interview where candidates are asked a number of prearranged questions in a specific order. The aim of this procedure is to standardise the interview procedure and make it as similar as possible for all candidates.

**task orientated** a style of leadership where the leader's priority is the completion of the task in hand rather than the interpersonal relationships in the group.

**test sophistication** a description of the process which occurs when individuals improve their scores on intelligence tests as a result of continuous practice. The individual becomes increasingly familiar with the type of problems used in a test and is able to answer more questions in a set time, causing their score on the test to improve.

**theory X** a set of assumptions which presume that work is not an activity that people enjoy. Theory X states that individuals must be coerced into performing well at work and will respond only to external threats and rewards.

**theory Y** a set of assumptions about the workforce which presume that work is an enjoyable activity and that individuals are self-motivated. They need a stimulating work environment and appreciate being led rather than driven.

**training-needs analysis** the process of analysing and describing the training needs in a company or organisation.

**trait** a stable and enduring personality characteristic.

**transfer of training** the effects on a new task of previous learning and skills. Transfer can be positive when skills from the first task assist in the performance of the second one, or negative when the skills from the first task inhibit the performance of the second one.

**unstructured interview** an interview which has no set format and often resembles an informal chat. The procedure will vary with each candidate.

**validity** the assumption that a test or assessment, such as a personality or intelligence test, is accurately measuring what it claims to be measuring.

    **face validity** the extent to which any test or assessment appears to be measuring what it claims to be measuring.

    **predictive validity** the capability of a test or assessment to predict future performance.

**weighted application blanks** application forms which are designed to meet the criteria drawn up by the use of biodata.

**white-collar** a term, originating in the USA used to describe non-manual workers.

# References

Argyle, M. (1988) Social relationships, in M. Hewstone, W. Stroebe, J. Codol and G.M. Stephenson (eds) *Introduction to Social Psychology*, Oxford: Blackwell.

Arvey, R.D. (1979) *Fairness in Selecting Employees*, Reading, MA: Addison-Wesley.

Asch, S.E. (1956) Studies of independence and conformity: a minority of one against a unanimous majority, *Psychological Monographs: General and Applied Psychology* 70, 1–70 (whole no. 416).

Atchley, R.C. (1991) *Social Forces and Ageing: an Introduction to Social Gerontology*, 6th edn, Belmont, CA: Wadsworth.

Atkinson, J.W. (1974) The mainsprings of achievement-orientated activity, in J.W. Atkinson and T.O. Raynor (eds) *Motivation and Achievement*, New York: Halstead.

Bales, R.F. (1950) *Interaction Process Analysis: A Method for the Study of Small Groups*, Cambridge, MA: Addison-Wesley.

Baltes, P.B. and Baltes, M.M. (1990) *Successful Ageing*, Cambridge: Cambridge University Press.

Baltes, P.B., Reece, H.W. and Lipsitt, L.P. (1990) Lifespan developmental psychology, *Annual Review of Psychology* 31, 65–110.

Bandura, A. (1974) Behaviour theory and models of man, *American Psychologist* 29, 859–69.

Banyard, P. (1996) *Applying Psychology to Health*, London: Hodder and Staughton.

Bavelas, A. (1950) Communication patterns in task-oriented groups, *Journal of the Acoustical Society of America* 22, 725–30.

Beale, N. and Nethercott, S. (1985) Job loss and family morbidity: a study of a factory closure, *Journal of the Royal College of General Practitioners* 35, 510–14.

Belbin, R.M. (1981) *Management Teams*, London: Heinemann.

Benson, P.L., Severs, D., Tatgeulorst, J. and Loddengard, N. (1980) The social costs of obesity: a non-reactive field trial, *Social Behaviour and Personality* 21, 75–87.

Blinkhorn, S. and Johnson, C. (1990) The insignificance of personality testing, *Nature* 348, 671–2.

Bradburn, N.M. (1969) *The Structure of Psychological Wellbeing*, Chicago: Aldine.

Breakwell, G.M. (1989) *Interviewing*, Leicester: British Psychological Society.

Brown, R. (1986) *Social Psychology. The Second Edition*, Free Press: New York.

Burawoy, M. (1979) *Manufacturing Consent: Changes in the Labour Process under Monopoly Capitalism*, Chicago: University of Chicago Press.

Carlson, N.R. (1988) *Discovering Psychology*, Needham Heights, MA: Allyn and Bacon

Carlson, N.R. and Buskist, W. (1997) *Psychology. The Science of Behaviour*, Needham Heights, MA: Allyn and Bacon.

Cattell, R.B. (1965) *The Scientific Analysis of Personality*, Harmondsworth, Middlesex: Penguin.

Cockburn, C. (1985) *Machinery of Dominance. Men, Women and Technical Knowledge*, London: Pluto Press.

Cooper, C.L. and Cartwright, S. (1995) Workplace stress; the primary approach, in O. Svane and C. Johansen (eds) *Work and Health. Scientific Basis of Progress in the Working Environment*, Luxembourg: European Commission.

Czeisler, C.A., Moore-Ede, M.C. and Coleman, R.M. (1982) Rotating shift work schedules that disrupt sleep are improved by applying circadian principles, *Science* 217, 460–3.

Dipboye, R.L. and Wiley, J.W. (1977) Reactions of college recruiters to interviewee sex and self presentation style, *Journal of Vocational Behaviour* 10, 1–12.

Dooley, C.D. and Catalano, R.A. (1984) The epidemiology of

economic stress, *American Journal of Community Psychology* 12, 387–409.

Drake, R.I. and Smith, P.J. (1973) *Behavioural Science in Industry*, Maidenhead: McGraw-Hill.

Dweck, C.S. (1986) Motivational processes affecting learning. Special issue. Psychological science and education, *American Psychologist* 1(10), 1040–8.

Eysenck, M. (ed.) (1998) *Psychology – an integrated approach*, Harlow: Addison Wesley Longman.

Feldman, D.C. (1976) A contingency theory of socialisation, *Administrative Science Quarterly* 21, 433–52.

Fiedler, F.E. (1967) *A Theory of Leadership Effectiveness*, New York: McGraw-Hill.

Freud, S. (1938) *The Basic Writings of Sigmund Freud* (J. Strachey ed. and trans.), New York: Norton.

Friedman, H.S., Tucker, J.S., Tomlinson-Keasey, C., Martin, L.R., Wingard, D.L. and Criqui, M.H. (1995) Psychosocial and behavioural predictors of longevity: the ageing and death of the 'Termites', *American Psychologist* 50, 69–78.

Fryer, D.M. and Payne, R.L. (1984) Proactivity in unemployment. Findings and implications, *Leisure Studies* 3, 273–95.

Furnham, A. (1990) *The Protestant Work Ethic*, London: Routledge.
—— (1997) *The Psychology of Behaviour at Work*, Guildford and Kings Lynn: Psychology Press.

Ghiselli, E.E. (1966) *The Validity of Occupational and Aptitude Tests*, New York: Wiley.

Goffman, I. (1961) *Asylums*, New York: Anchor Books.

Goldsmith, D. (1922) The use of the personal history blank as a salesmanship test, *Journal of Applied Psychology* 6, 149–55.

Green, R.G. (1991) Social motivation, *Annual Review of Psychology* 42, 377–99.

*Guardian* (1999) *The Guardian and Observer Newspapers on CD-ROM*, London: Chadwyck-Healey.

Halpin, A.W. and Winer, B.H. (1952) *The Leadership Behaviour of the Airplane Commander*, Colombus, OH: Ohio State University Research Foundation.

Hawkins, L.H. and Armstrong-Esther, C.A. (1978) Circadian rhythms and night shift working in nurses, *Nursing Times*, May 4, 49–52.

Health Education Authority (1988) 78 New Oxford Street, London WC1A 1AH.

Herriot, P. (1981) *Assessment and Selection in Organisations*, Chichester: Wiley.

Herzberg, F. (1966) *Work and the Nature of Man*, Chicago: World Publishing Co.

HMSO (1998 and 1999) *British Social Attitudes Survey*, Social Trends, London.

Holmes, T.H. and Rahe, R.H. (1967) The social readjustment rating scale. *Journal of Psycho-somatic Research* 11 213–18.

Jahoda, M. (1958) *Work, Employment and Unemployment. A Social Psychological Analysis*, Cambridge: Cambridge University Press.

Jahoda, M., Lazarfield, P.F. and Zeisel, H. (1933) *Marienthal. The Sociography of an Unemployed Community*. English translation 1971, Aldine-Atherton: New York.

Janis, I.L. (1982) *Groupthink: Psychological Studies of Policy Decisions and Fiascos* (2nd edn), Boston, MA: Houghton-Mifflin.

Jessup, G. and Jessup, H. (1971) Validity of the EPI in pilot selection, *Occupational Psychology* 45(2), 111–23.

Katz, A.M. (1978) Job longevity as a situational factor in job satisfaction, *Administrative Science Quarterly* 23, 204–23.

Kerr, N.L. and Bray, R.M. (eds) (1982) *The Psychology of the Courtroom*, London: Academic Press.

Kobasa, S.C. (1982) The hardy personality. Toward a social psychology of stress and health, in G. Sanders and J. Sub (eds) *Social Psychology of Health and Illness*, Hillsdale, NJ: Erlbaum.

Koestner, R. and McClelland, D.C. (1990) Perspectives on competence motivation, in L.A. Pavin (ed.) *Handbook of Personality Theory and Research*, New York: Guilford Press.

Lamm, H. and Myers, D.G. (1978) Group induced polarization of attitudes and behaviour, in L. Beskowitz (ed.) *Advances in Experimental Social Psychology* vol. 11, New York: Academic Press.

Landy, F.J. (1985) *Psychology of Work Behaviour*, 3rd edn, Homewood, IL: Dorsey Press.

Larkin, J. and Pines, H. (1979) No fat person need apply, *Sociology of Work and Occupations* 6, 312–27.

Latane, B., Williams, K.D. and Hawkins, S.G. (1979) Many hands make light the work: the causes and consequences of social loafing, *Journal of Personality and Social Psychology* 22, 822–32.

Latham, G.P. and Saari, L.M. (1979) Application of social learning theory to training supervisors through behavioural modelling, *Journal of Applied Psychology* 64, 239–46.

Lazarus, R.S. and Folkman, S. (1984) *Stress, Appraisal and Coping*, New York: Springer.

Lewin, K., Lippett, R. and White, R. (1939) Patterns of aggressive behaviour in experimentally created social climates, *Journal of Social Psychology* 10, 271–99.

Marmot, M.G. and Rose, E. (1981) Social class and coronary heart disease, *British Medical Journal* 45, 13–19.

Marmot, M.G., Dowey-Smith, G., Stansfield, S., Patel, C., North, F., Head, J., *et al.* (1982) Health inequalities among British civil servants – the Whitehall Study, *The Lancet* 337, 1387–93.

Maslow, A. (1954) *Motivation and Personality*, New York: Van Nostrand Reinhold.

Maslow, A.H. (1970) A theory of human motivation, *Psychological Review* 50, 370–96.

Mayfield, E.C. (1964) The selection interview: a re-evaluation of research, *Personnel Psychology* 17, 239–60.

McClelland, D.C. (1965) Achievement and entrepreneurship: a longtitudinal study, *Journal of Personality and Social Psychology* 1, 389–92.

—— (1985) *Human Motivation*, Glenview, IL: Scott, Foresman.

McGregor, D. (1960) *The Human Side of Enterprise*, New York: McGraw-Hill.

Michelini, R.L. and Snodgrass, S.R. (1980) Defendant characteristics and juridical decisions, *Journal of Research in Personality* 14, 340–50.

Miller, C.E. (1989) The social psychological effects of group decision rules, in P.B. Paulus (ed.) *Psychology of Group Influence* 2nd edn, pp. 327–56, Hillsdale, NJ: Erlbaum.

Moser, K.A., Fox, A.J. and Jones, D.R. (1984) Unemployment and mortality in the OPCS longitudinal study, *The Lancet* 1, 365–7.

Pavlov, I.P. (1927) *Conditioned Reflexes*, London: Oxford University Press.

Perrin, S. and Spencer, C. (1981) Independence or conformity in the Asch experiment as a reflection of cultural and situational factors, *British Journal of Social Psychology* 20, 205–9.

Porteous, M. (1997) *Occupational Psychology*, Hemel Hemstead: Prentice Hall.

Raven, J.C. (1965) *Ravens Progressive Matrices*, London: H.K. Lewis.

Rice, R.W. (1978) Construct validity of the least preferred co-worker score, *Psychological Bulletin* 85,1192–275.

Riggio, E.R. (1990) *Introduction to Industrial Organisational Psychology*, Glenview, IL: Scott Foresman.

Ringlemann, M. (1913) Recherches sur les moteurs animées: travail de l'homme, *Annales de l'Institute National Agronomique* 2(12), 1–40.

Roy, D.F. (1960) Banana time: job satisfaction and informal interaction, *Human Organisation* 18, 156–68.

Seabrook, J. (1982) *Unemployment*, London: Quartet Books.

Selye, H. (1956) *The Stress of Life*, New York: McGraw-Hill.

Skinner, B.F. (1938) *The Behaviour of Organisms*, New York: Appleton-Century-Crofts.

Statt, D.A. (1994) *Psychology and the World of Work*, Basingstoke: Macmillan.

Stogdill, R. (1974) *Handbook of Leadership*, New York: Free Press.

Stoner, J.A.F. (1961) 'A Comparison of Individual and Group Decisions including Risk', unpublished Masters thesis, MITT.

Tajfel, H. (1978) Intergroup behaviour: Individualistic perspectives, in H. Tajfel and C. Fraser (eds) *Introducing Social Psychology*, Harmondsworth: Penguin.

Tajfel, H. and Turner, J.C. (1979) An integrative theory of intergroup conflict, in W.G. Austin and S. Worchel (eds) *The Social Psychology of Intergroup Relationships*, pp. 33–47, Monterey, CA: Brooks/ Cole.

Taylor, F.W. (1911) *The Principles of Scientific Management*, New York: Harper.

Terman, L.M. and Oden, H.M. (1947) *The Gifted Child Grows Up. Volume 4. Genetic Studies of Genius*, Stanford, CA: Stanford University Press.

Thorndike, E.L. (1898) Animal intelligence: an experimental study of the associative process in animals, *Psychological Review*, Monograph Supplement 2 (whole no. 8).

Townsend, P. (1957) *The Family Life of Old People*, London: Routledge.

Tripplet, N. (1898) The dynamogenic factors in pacemaking and competition, *American Journal of Psychology* 9, 507–33.

Tuckman, B.W. (1965) Developmental sequences in small groups, *Psychological Bulletin* 63, 384–99.

Warr, P.B. (1987) *Work, Unemployment and Mental Health*, Oxford: Oxford Science Publications.

Warr, P.B. and Jackson, P.B. (1985) Factors influencing the psychological impact of prolonged unemployment and reemployment, *Psychological Medicine* 15, 795–807.

Wechsler, D. (1955) *Manual for the Wechsler Adult Intelligence Scale*, San Antonio: The Psychological Corporation.

Wilkinson, R.G. (1986) Income and mortality, in R.G. Wilkinson (ed.) *Class and Health: Research and Longtitudinal Data*, London: Tavistock.

Williams, D., Karau, S.J. and Bourgeios, M. (1993) Working on collective tasks: social loafing and social compensation, in M.A. Hogg and D. Abrams (eds) *Group Motivation: Social Psychological Perspectives*, pp. 130–48, London: Harvester-Wheatsheaf.

Yuki, G. (1981) *Leadership in Organisations*, Engelwood Cliffs, NJ: Prentice Hall.

Zahrani, S.S. and Kaplowitz, S.A. (1993) Attributional biases in individualistic and collectivist cultures: a comparison of Americans with Saudis, *Social Psychology Quarterly* 56(3), 223–33.

Zajonc, R.B. (1965) Social facilitation, *Science* 149, 269–74.

# Index

Bold page numbers refer to the Glossary.